THIS NAKED MIND: NICOTINE

THIS NAKED MIND:
NICOTINE

The Science-Based Method to Reclaim Your Health and Take Control Easily

ANNIE GRACE AND WILLIAM PORTER

AVERY

an imprint of Penguin Random House

New York

AVERY

an imprint of Penguin Random House LLC
penguinrandomhouse.com

Illustrations by This Naked Mind, LLC

Most Avery books are available at special quantity discounts for bulk purchase for sales promotions, premiums, fund-raising, and educational needs. Special books or book excerpts also can be created to fit specific needs. For details, write SpecialMarkets@penguinrandomhouse.com.

Library of Congress Cataloging-in-Publication Data

Names: Grace, Annie, 1978– author.
Title: This naked mind: nicotine: the science-based method to reclaim
your health and take control easily / Annie Grace and William Porter.
Description: New York: Avery, an imprint of Penguin Random House, [2022]
Identifiers: LCCN 2022008257 (print) | LCCN 2022008258 (ebook) |
ISBN 9780593539477 (trade paperback) | ISBN 9780593539484 (epub)
Subjects: LCSH: Nicotine addiction—Treatment. | Substance abuse. |
Tobacco use—Psychological aspects.
Classification: LCC RC567.G72 2022 (print) |
LCC RC567 (ebook) | DDC 616.86/5—dc23/eng/20220322
LC record available at https://lccn.loc.gov/2022008257
LC ebook record available at https://lccn.loc.gov/2022008258

Printed in the United States of America
1st Printing

Book design by Laura K. Corless

For everyone who has found the courage to break free,
and has helped free others by spreading the word

ThisNakedMindNicotine.com
AlcoholExplained.com

Contents

Contents

Preface

I n 2013, we were two professional people struggling with addiction. Annie, a C-level marketing executive from the US, found her daily drinking was becoming increasingly unmanageable. William, a lawyer from the UK, had found that his weekend binges were becoming longer, more intense, and increasingly difficult to recover from.

On the face of it we had very little in common other than our drinking problem, but our struggle would eventually bring us into partnership. We both felt an urgency to bring a solution to the thousands of people suffering, and help them believe that addiction can be rationalized, understood, and above all, beaten.

Both heavily influenced by the late Allen Carr, we expanded on his theories of addiction using our own knowledge and experience. We each found true freedom and wrote books about our methods and our journey. Annie's books, *This Naked Mind* and *The Alcohol Experiment*, and William's book, *Alcohol Explained*, have become seminal works on alcohol addiction. Many people use our books together when they are seeking to change their relationship with alcohol. We scaled the same mountain, but just via different routes.

We have heard from our readers that they are eager for us to apply our methods to nicotine, which for some can be an even more complex, addictive relationship. This book is our answer: a groundbreaking, science-based program combining our deep research and experience to address all forms of nicotine addiction. The personal stories are grounded in William's experience smoking, vaping, and dipping. William managed to quit with the help of Allen Carr's quit-smoking books, but it was a long and arduous process. Our method builds on the principles behind Allen Carr's books, but it leads to more immediate, lasting change. Let's get started.

Introduction:
The Beginning of the Shift

The alarm goes off. I feel tired and groggy, but immediately a positive thought enters my head, one that gets me moving even though I'm still half asleep: I can get up and light a cigarette. I get up, grab the cigarettes, and head outside. It's freezing cold but I don't care; the pleasure of that first cigarette of the day far outweighs any minor feeling of discomfort caused by the cold. I light up and take a lungful of smoke.

The taste of the tobacco and the feel of the smoke going into my lungs is wonderful. I immediately feel calmer, more confident, more in control. Everyone knows that smoking kills you, but what non-smokers don't appreciate is the great pleasure in smoking. That feeling of peace and tranquility and confidence that comes when you have a cigarette. I've smoked for years and I've tried to stop more times than I can count, and I've just never managed it. The problem is that the pleasure outweighs the risk. The effect on my health worries me, the sore throat worries me, the coughing worries me. My general lack of fitness worries me. The cost worries me. But stopping just doesn't seem to be a viable option for me. Not because I don't see the harms but, to be honest, because *I don't truly want to stop.*

The last time I tried to stop I was watching TV, some ridiculous sitcom, and it was infuriating me. The stupid characters, the ridiculous story line, the pathetic jokes. Eventually I just couldn't take any more. I rushed out, got a packet of cigarettes, and sat there and lit one up. Suddenly that ridiculous sitcom didn't bother me in the least. I sat there as happy as anything with my cigarette, even beginning to enjoy the idiocy on the television.

This sums up my life as a smoker. While a part of me feared what it was doing to me, I just couldn't imagine enjoying life without smoking. Being unable to quit, for me, felt less like a failure of willpower and more like a rational decision. Life just wasn't the same without it. Whatever its downsides, it was a necessity rather than a luxury.

Why would I opt for a half life, a miserable life, a life spent wanting something I couldn't have? A life without my regular release from the daily grind? Where I didn't have a little something to lift me up over the never-ending stream of daily frustrations? That little something that stopped me worrying about all the irritating nonsense that life kept throwing at me?

I knew lots of non-smokers, and they exercised and ate healthily. They were people who didn't seem to care about quality of life. Who didn't value sitting back and enjoying the moment. People who would sacrifice quality of their daily lives in order to add a few more years onto their life span. Very simply, they were people who seemed to have very different priorities than mine. I want to enjoy life, to have the ability to sit back and let all the aggravations wash over me without affecting me. For me, smoking was the difference between enjoying life and suffering it.

This is why quitting tobacco is so difficult. Whether you smoke, vape, dip, or chew, it tastes good. It makes you feel good. It gives you a few moments out of the day to rise above the daily grind and just enjoy the moment. It gives you the confidence to deal with all the stresses and strains of everyday life. It gives you confidence when you're socializing. It helps you relax. It's a companion when you're alone. It helps you concentrate when you need to, and it gives you something to do when you're bored.

And all the while it gives you a little emotional boost and provides a shield against all the stresses and strains of life.

But let's imagine differently for a moment. What if it didn't do any of those things? What if it tasted foul, and didn't make you feel good—at all? What if it didn't relax you or give you confidence? What if it actually prevented you from concentrating, and caused you to be bored?

Imagine if it felt unpleasant every time you did it? Imagine if it robbed you of energy and left you feeling tired and heavy and weak. Imagine if every dose took you from feeling confident and happy and relaxed, and made you feel heavy and tired and depressed.

If that were the case, then quitting wouldn't be hard work, it wouldn't take effort, and success would come easily. It would be a simple and natural progression, from being a smoker (or vaper or dipper) to not being one. There would be no willpower involved because willpower is about resisting temptation. But if you didn't want it, actually had *no desire* for a smoke or a vape, then there would be no temptation. And nothing to resist.

It may seem hard to believe, and it is OK to be skeptical, but this new understanding is what gave me the key to quitting smoking. I enjoyed (or rather I believed that I enjoyed) smoking, but I hated what it was doing to me. I hated the constant coughing, the sore throat after a heavy night, the constant worry about the long-term health effects, the fact that I was literally burning money. I hated (even though I didn't truly appreciate) the effect it had on my physical health, but most of all I hated the fact that I didn't understand it! I didn't understand why I continued to desire it— *despite knowing the downside.* I didn't understand why other people seemed just fine without it, yet I couldn't even go a few hours without one; why some people could go through life without ever having to smoke, yet for me it was a necessity. All of these things bothered me. Sometimes I could ignore them, sometimes I couldn't, but whether I ignored them or not they were never far away.

So how do you get from the one state of mind to the other? How do you change your perception so that quitting is no longer hard work? That is the purpose of this book. You may feel extremely cynical when you read this; after all, you know for a fact that smoking tastes good and helps you relax, so how can it be otherwise? You have personal experience that confirms these truths. You may believe that no amount of positive mantras or platitudes are going to convince you otherwise, no smooth-talking "sales pitch" is going to convince you that you don't enjoy smoking, or convince you that you won't be miserable without it.

All I ask of you is to move forward with an open mind. This isn't a book about mantras or platitudes or an inner child or anything so ethereal or insubstantial. It is a book based on common sense and science. We are going to take your hand and lead you on a journey of discovery, we're going to deconstruct your smoking and vaping habits, we're going to tear it all down and examine every last bit of it and see if it really is what you currently think it is, or if perhaps it might be something very different from your current perception of it.

Imagine that you're living in a beautiful house, a mansion, and you're very happy there. At least you were to begin with, but over the years it has started to show signs of wear and tear. The wallpaper is beginning to fade, the paintwork looks marked and scruffy, but far more worrying is that the bricks look like they're starting to crumble. You think some of the pipes or the roof may be leaking because there's moisture in some areas and this seems to be causing you some health issues. You've seen quite a few cracks in some of the walls, and perhaps worst of all you've heard rustling in some of the rooms (mice? rats? cockroaches?).

Fortunately you know a great carpenter. Someone who can take you through your house and explain exactly what you're up against. They're going to pull up the drains, look under the carpets and behind the wallpaper, check the roof and the pipes and the woodwork, and you're going to follow them around every step of the way so they can explain it all to you: what the problems are, what has caused them, what can (or can't) be done about them. When you have all that information and knowledge you can make a simple decision: do you want to keep it as it is? Or give it a complete overhaul?

That is what we're going to do in this book with your smoking habits. We are going to deconstruct the entire phenomenon of smoking, vaping, chewing, and dipping. We are going to look at the human body and brain to see how it affects us, what it does for us, and (crucially) what it doesn't do for us. We are going to break the entire thing down into its constituent parts and examine each and every one of those parts, so that by the end you have all the information you need to make a simple decision: how you move forward in your relationship with nicotine. You can make a decision based on common sense and knowledge, rather than fear. After all, for many people, it is fear that keeps them smoking; fear that their life will never be quite so enjoyable when they quit; that smoking is such an integral part of who they are that they will be losing a part of their very character when they quit.

If you are still smoking, vaping, or chewing, you can and should continue to do so while reading this book (in the same way as if, when looking at the quality of your house, it would be more effective if you determined everything that was wrong, along with your carpenter, before starting to make repairs, and crucially while you were still living there!). On the other hand, if you've already quit there is no need to start again (after all, if you've already moved out of your house and found somewhere better, but are doubting whether the move was the right choice, the builder could point out the problems with your old home without you first having to move back in, to help you solidify your decision and to stop second-guessing it).

In some chapters in this book you will find Engagement Points. These are short, practical exercises that help consolidate the information and ideas covered in the chapter. It is possible with a book to read and understand it on an intellectual level, without then applying it to your personal experiences. These Engagement Points really help you apply the ideas and concepts to your smoking experiences in a very practical way. You do not have to work through them, but they can help you consolidate your new perspective on smoking.

There is a quote, often attributed to Benjamin Franklin, that goes: "Tell me and I forget, teach me and I may remember, involve me and I learn."

This isn't a book that expects you to take what we say for granted. This is a book that invites you to consider a new perspective. You do this by listening to what we say, evaluating its worth, then checking out its validity with reference to your experiences. Engagement Points are designed to assist you with this.

1.

This Naked Mind:
How and Why the Method Works

We human beings like to think that we're rational creatures, that our decisions and actions are based on common sense and rational thought. But the fact is that our minds are made up of both conscious and subconscious parts, and the subconscious part plays a huge role in our decision-making processes.

Your brain actually automates a lot of the activities you engage in on a day-to-day basis, and I'm not just talking about things like your heartbeat or breathing, I'm talking about physical actions we take on a day-to-day basis, like punching in a password or turning lights on or off or driving.

Think about if you wanted to learn juggling. You buy three balls, you maybe get a pamphlet on how to start, or you watch a few videos on You-Tube. Then what? You don't just start juggling perfectly. You throw the balls in the air, try to juggle them, and drop them. And drop them again. And again. Then suddenly you manage to catch one before dropping them. Then you manage to catch one and flip it into the air before the next one lands. Then you manage two. Then three. Slowly, and with practice, you get the hang of it.

Think about these words that we use so often without ever really stopping to think about their implications: "practice" and "getting the hang" of something. Words and phrases so simple we never stop to analyze them. Think about learning to juggle. What is actually going on? You have a skeleton with muscles attached to it and by contracting, the muscles can make the skeleton move. Learning to juggle is a complicated coordination between hundreds of different muscles, getting your hands in exactly the right place at the right time depending on the weight and size of the balls, the pull of gravity, the effects of air pressure, and a thousand other delicate calculations.

The point here is that the student juggler doesn't need to sit down with a pen and paper and work out the weight of the ball, the gravitational force, air drag, muscle contraction, timing, and all the other things that are required to juggle. They just throw the balls again and again and again, and under the level of their conscious mind an amazing thing is going on. The subconscious is coordinating the whole process. It recognizes every time something goes wrong, every time something gets better, and makes infinitesimal adjustments all the time. When something goes well it learns to repeat the sequence, and when something goes badly it rejects it and makes adjustments. With constant repeated attempts, these improvements are made. We start off useless, we slowly improve, we become competent, then proficient, then expert.

This isn't just true for juggling, it's true of any physical activity. Not just sports like football, baseball, hockey, motor racing, or learning to ride a bike. Soldiers aren't just shown how to load and fire a weapon, then sent out to the battlefield to get on with it. They are shown, and then practice the process again and again until they're stripping and loading their weapon in their sleep. Then, when they are in the chaos of battle, with the exhaustion and fear and shock, they react automatically. Those rounds just keep flying toward the enemy. Think of the word *experience.* It's doing something over and over again so you get better at it.

The subconscious doesn't just learn, it remembers. Think of the phrase, "it's like riding a bike." It takes time and practice to learn to ride a bike, but when you've learned how to do it (or rather, when your subconscious has worked out the exact muscle coordination required to ride it) it's not something you ever forget. This is good in one respect but can be bad in another. After all, what if what's been learned suddenly needs to be changed? This is a specifically modern problem. When we were cave dwellers there were very few motor responses that would suddenly become obsolete and need to be changed. After all, our muscular structure remains fairly constant, as does our skeleton, gravity, air drag, and so forth. But modern living has thrown up some interesting challenges.

Anyone who has worked with a computer that requires them to change their password will find that for a few days after they've changed their password they'll be punching in the old one every time they try to log in. Similarly, if you've ever experienced a power outage you may find yourself constantly walking into dark rooms and instinctively flipping the light switch even though you know there's an outage. Force of habit, right? If you're a driver and you find yourself in a car as a passenger with someone who is driving too fast and too close to the car in front, you may find your right leg tensing as your subconscious mind tries to apply the brake and slow the vehicle down. There isn't a brake on the passenger side of the car, but this isn't a conscious decision, it's your subconscious kicking in and tensing your right leg because experience and repetition has taught it that that is what you need to do to slow down a vehicle.

So a lot of our decision-making is automated and takes place in the subconscious. On one level this is great, it frees up our conscious mind to deal with more complicated things; the things that need more thought and consideration. It allows our subconscious to handle the smaller, repetitive tasks like chewing gum or blinking dust out of our eyes. Similar to the role of CEO of a big company—it is not efficient for he or she to micromanage everything, so decisions get delegated down the chain of command. The simple decisions, the no-brainers, happen way underneath the boss's line of sight.

The system works beautifully if all the information that the subconscious is using to make decisions is accurate. The problem is that sometimes the information running the automatic decisions is full of errors, and we don't even know it. It's kind of like when that car you are a passenger in is going too fast. The subconscious works on cause and effect: tense right leg, vehicle slows down. It isn't capable of factoring in all the relevant considerations, such as the fact that there needs to be a brake under your right foot in order for this to work. It is operating automatically with errors in the information.

So if your subconscious is making certain decisions for you, but has incomplete or incorrect information, you can expect to keep on making the same decisions—ones that you might not be entirely happy about. So what do you do about it? In fact, it's fairly simple: you take back control. Your conscious mind can override your subconscious, in the same way that the boss of the company can decide that he or she no longer wants the administrative assistant making strategic decisions about the direction the company is taking.

This is a two-step process. First you open up your subconscious and consciously examine everything that's in there. You discard what is incorrect and factor in anything that's relevant to a decision but isn't currently being taken into account. Imagine you've got an attic or garage full of dusty old boxes that you haven't opened in a decade. From day to day it's not a major problem, but you're kind of aware of it at the back of your mind. It's one of those jobs that needs doing that you just never get around to. So what do you do? You put a day aside and you drag everything out, blow the dust off it, and examine the contents of every single box. If there's something in there that's broken or useless, you get rid of it. If there's something in there that's useful, you take it out and actually use it. You no longer have a lot of useless stuff that you don't know anything about; you have a clear and tidy space and some genuinely useful stuff back in your life.

So there are subconscious decisions, but of course there are also conscious decisions. These are exactly what you'd expect them to be—things we think about. With them, we weigh the pros and cons and come to the best decision we can, based on all available information. This is all well and good, but you need to be sure of three things. First, is the information you have correct? Second, is it relevant? Third, is there anything important that you're missing?

When we are considering whether something is correct, we need to factor in the idea that reality and our perception of reality are not always the same thing. Our perception of reality is based on our experience and observations, upon which we form assumptions, then draw conclusions, then form beliefs. These beliefs are our "reality," but they may not be an objective reality, and they can be changed.

Liminal thinking is a method developed by author Dave Gray. Liminal thinking defines how, through the conscious exploration and acceptance of new ideas and truths, you can influence your subconscious mind. It gives you back your ability to make rational and logical decisions about smoking, no longer influenced by illogical, incorrect, emotional, or irrational desires. It gives you control and freedom by changing your understanding of, and therefore your relationship with, smoking.

Perhaps you've heard the ancient story about the blind men and the elephant. Three blind men are brought into a room with an elephant, and each man touches a different part. One touches the tail, one the trunk, and one the side. When asked what they are touching, they begin to argue. The one touching the trunk believes he is touching a snake; the one touching the body, a wall; and the one touching the tail, a rope.

Each blind man is saying what he believes to be true. And each man's experience proves it, because we tend to trust our experiences implic-itly. Of course, the truth is that none of them are correct. They are all experiencing a piece of reality and forming their own, very different, opinions.

Gray explains that we only see and experience part of reality, and no matter how many experiences we have had, our brains are not powerful enough to experience and observe everything. Gray makes the point that we are limited by what we pay attention to: "In any given moment, the more you focus on one aspect of your experience, the less you notice ev-erything else." We usually notice only the things specific to our immedi-ate reality: the society we grew up in, the media, the influencers in our lives, and our actual life experiences.

Gray states that upon those relevant experiences and observations we make assumptions, from those assumptions we draw conclusions, and from those conclusions we form beliefs. Gray defines belief as everything we "know" to be true.

This illustration demonstrates that the things we "know" to be true are not actually formed by reality, but by reality as we have interpreted it through our experiences, observations, assumptions, and conclusions. Consider how this applies to smoking. Collectively held beliefs are not built directly on the foundation of reality.

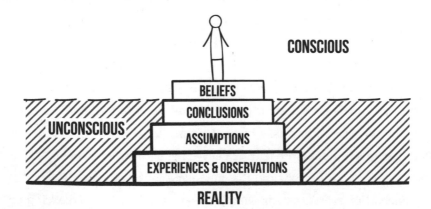

Consider the following statements:

- Smoking helps me relax.
- Smoking gives me confidence.
- Smoking helps me concentrate.
- Smoking helps me socialize.
- I enjoy smoking.
- I can't stop smoking.
- Smoking is a part of who I am.
- Smoking helps me deal with stress.
- Certain situations just aren't quite the same without a cigarette.

We think of these things as facts, but are they?

Have you ever gone to a doctor with an ailment, and been asked to give your pain a score on a 1 to 10 scale? Did you know that your mood will affect this score? Two people may have the same medical complaint, identical in every way. If one person is otherwise happy, content with their life and satisfied with their life, they'll give a lower pain score than if they were miserable and struggling. Two people have an identical knee injury. One of them has just won the lottery and found the love of their life. The other has just lost their job and is going through a bad breakup. The first person is likely to give the pain a 2 out of 10. The second is going to give it a 7. Our perception of reality is not necessarily reality, particularly when feelings and emotions are thrown into the mix.

Beliefs can be particularly difficult to change, for several reasons. One reason is that we subconsciously self-seal them by seeking out anything that appears to support them. This is called confirmation bias, the tendency to search for or interpret information in a way that confirms one's preconceptions. Over time these beliefs become so ingrained in our minds (and in our society), and so repeatedly self-sealed, that they are programmed into our subconscious. By definition the subconscious is not readily accessible or easily changed. We need a specific process with which to dive into the foundation of our beliefs, examine them, and change our perceived reality.

This book is designed to give you control and freedom by changing your understanding of, and therefore your relationship with, nicotine. While tradition, advertising, and societal norms condition our subconscious to believe that nicotine is beneficial in some ways (for example, by helping us relax and rise above the stresses and strains of everyday life), this book will expose that subconscious conditioning and recondition your subconscious.

So what can we do? How can we explore reality and change our subconscious beliefs about smoking? It's relatively simple. We need to bring subconscious experiences, observations, assumptions, and conclusions into conscious thought. This allows your subconscious to change. The concept is scientifically proven—scientists now realize that the brain is able to change and adapt in response to new experiences, in a process called neuroplasticity.

The process of illuminating your subconscious foundation of belief will influence your subconscious mind. To do this, we will logically and critically provide you with information about smoking, vaping, dipping, chewing, and nicotine. We will expose your beliefs, assumptions, and conclusions by presenting you with methodical, factual, and rational arguments for you to question and evaluate. You'll be completely in control: you'll be the judge as we strip away misinformation and present new concepts you have not yet critically considered. We will give you the tools to discover your truth, your reality, and the ability to understand that the rope you are holding that you think is your lifeline, might really be the tail of a poisonous snake.

This is how this book works. It gives you a complete reevaluation of all the factors that go into your decision to smoke, both conscious and subconscious.

Before we try a cigarette for the first time we don't need to smoke. We enjoy life, we socialize, we cope with stress, we concentrate on things, we get through bouts of boredom, all without needing to smoke. But then we start smoking, and we learn to *enjoy* it. Then it's kind of like we enter an alternative reality, one where we can't imagine enjoying life in quite the same way again without having that little reward to punctuate our day. For many people, this is one of the main barriers to stopping—the inability to imagine a full and happy life without smoking.

ENGAGEMENT POINT

Make a list of the benefits of smoking. Yes, you heard me right. Forget all the downsides for a minute and make a list of what you enjoy about it, the ways in which it seems to help. You may end up with things like:

I enjoy it.
It helps me relax.
It's a little reward to look forward to.
It helps me concentrate.
It helps me deal with stress.
It helps me socialize.
It's something to do when I'm bored.
Life isn't quite the same without it.

Keep this list close, and keep referring to it throughout the book.

2.

The Smoker or the Cigarette?
Part 1: The Smoker

One of the main definitions of life is "the ability to respond to external stimuli," and in particular to the environment that the living thing finds itself in. All living things have the ability to adapt; this allows them to survive and thrive in an ever-changing environment. The more complicated the life-form, the more intricate is its ability to adapt.

One of the most obvious forms of this ability to adapt is in relation to food. We humans know what we can and can't eat because our food is carefully packaged and labeled, and things that might poison us are very clearly marked as poison and their sales restricted. But what about animals? Their food isn't packaged. How do they know what to eat and what not to eat? They don't have labeling, or nutritionists, to tell them what to eat and what to avoid, so how do they manage?

Where Annie lives in Colorado, they have bears. People need to keep their trash cans locked away to stop the bears from going through them looking for food. But they need to leave the cans out once a week so the trash can be collected. And of course, that's when the bears come along. The trash ends up strewn all over the yard. Well, some of it does. The dirty diapers, the used tea bags, the empty packets. The rest of it, the left-over spaghetti, pizza, meat, that all gets eaten. The bears just go through the can, eat the food, and throw the rest all over the yard. In London, we have a similar, if slightly less dramatic, issue with foxes. But how do bears and foxes know what to eat and what to leave? No one has ever sat them down and explained the nutritional benefits of leftover roast beef com-pared to, say, a dirty diaper.

In fact, it's very simple: animals use their sense of smell and taste. If something smells good to them, they eat it. If it doesn't, they don't. So, leaves smell and taste good to a giraffe, to a lion of the smell of an ante-lope makes them hungry, and so on. It's a nice simple setup, and it works. But it's a lot more complicated than just our genes being programmed to like certain things and to dislike others. After all, living beings need to adapt in order to survive. If you are a monkey and are happy eating figs, but there's a disease that breaks out killing lots of the fig trees, you have to start eating something else or you'll starve. So how does a monkey make this shift?

First, there's hunger. The hungrier a living thing gets, the more des-perate it will become to eat, and this desperation will cause it to try eat-ing many different types of food. When people or animals are starving they will eat virtually anything as they become increasingly desperate.

Going back to our monkey analogy, say you've spent many happy years eating figs, but now the figs are becoming rarer and rarer. There are lots of other berries and fruits, but which ones are poison and which ones are beneficial? You're not human, you cannot google "edible berries," and you cannot ask a nutritionist what to do. So, nature runs its course. As you become hungrier and hungrier, you become increasingly desperate and eventually your natural reluctance to try something new, something that could be poisonous, is overridden by your desperation. You take a berry and you eat it.

This is something you've never eaten before, so it tastes strange, different, unfamiliar. Things can then go one of two ways. Either the berry is poison, in which case you're going to be ill for a bit and shortly after eating you will start to feel far worse, or it has some nutritional value, in which case you will immediately feel better—after all, if you are desperately hungry and you eat something nutritious, you will immediately feel a boost as the energy and nutrients flood into your system.

But here's the clever bit: the subconscious part of the brain will reinterpret the taste in light of the effect. If a taste is followed by an unpleasant experience, your subconscious will make sure you avoid that taste in the future. If a taste is followed by a good feeling, the subconscious will cause you to want to seek out the taste again.

This is essentially what an "acquired taste" is. We may find the taste of something strange of unpleasant to begin with, but with repeated exposure to it (and providing it has an apparent positive effect on us), we come to "enjoy" the taste. The taste doesn't change, but the way our brain interprets that taste does. "Warning, stay away, poison" eventually changes to "this helps us, seek it out."

This ability to adapt is one of the greatest survival mechanisms of life on this planet. It's a fantastic system and it works extremely well, but the problem is that it is confused by drugs and ends up working against us. Drugs have an apparent (but false) benefit in that they make us feel better, but they are in fact poison. One of the easiest ways of seeing this is with dipping tobacco.

For those not familiar with it, dipping tobacco is a very finely shredded, moist tobacco that you take a pinch of and you put in your mouth between your gum and your cheek. It gives you a fairly good kick of nicotine, but over time can cause mouth cancer and may burn its way right through the cheek.

Wait, what? How on earth does that work? If you are putting something against your skin that eventually burns through your cheek, doesn't it hurt? Doesn't it burn and sting? I spent many years dipping and I can say absolutely that it does burn and it does sting. But here's the amazing (and very worrying) thing: because your subconscious brain interprets the *effect* (which is the dose of nicotine) as positive, it starts to reevaluate the *cause* (in this case the burning, stinging sensation) as also positive. Over time, that burning sensation feels warming, sweet, piquant. Again, as with food, the feeling hasn't changed, but how our brain interprets it has. Isn't that both amazing and horrible? How our brains can be fooled into interpreting something extremely damaging as enjoyable because of the confusing effects of a drug?

If you've never been addicted to dipping tobacco you may find this difficult to believe. But stop for a minute. Is it any different than breathing cancerous smoke or vapor into your lungs? Do you think that any creature on the planet that relies on inhaling oxygen to survive is naturally designed to breathe in a poison, day in, day out, until it eventually kills it? Don't most people, when they try a cigarette (or even a vape) for the first time, cough and splutter and have to learn to "enjoy" it? Breathing cancerous fumes into your lungs is not pleasant and the immediate reaction of the body is to be repulsed by it and to reject it. It usually does this by inducing coughing—forcibly ejecting the smoke from the lungs in the quickest, most effective way possible. It is only over time, and with repeated use, that the brain is eventually fooled into thinking that the act of breathing in smoke or nicotine-laden vapor is pleasurable, because the effect (the dose of nicotine) appears to be beneficial. Your body subdues the natural coughing reaction in order to obtain the "benefit" of the effect of a dose of nicotine. A natural survival mechanism is overridden.

The question is: what is it that nicotine does to us that is so great that our brains will override our natural defense mechanism, allowing it to cripple and even kill us?

3.

The Smoker or the Cigarette?
Part 2: The Cigarette

People smoke in full knowledge that it is hugely harmful to their health, but most of us make the excuse that we'll stop before it kills us, or that (for whatever reason) the ill effects of smoking aren't going to get us like it gets other people. I've had people tell me that they're OK to smoke because they don't eat meat, that they live in the country where the air is cleaner, and that they don't smoke enough for it to be a threat to them. These days, as the health effects become harder and harder to avoid knowing, the usual refuge of the smoker, when confronted by all the health scares, may say, "Well, you've got to die of something" (which is true, but all deaths aren't created equal; compare, for example, dying in your forties from a crashing heart attack or lung cancer, compared to dying in your sleep in your eighties). But what about all the people each year who are told by their doctor that they have reached the point where they are going to die imminently, that if they don't quit they will be dead in a few months? What about the people who are told this and yet still continue to smoke?

Cigarette smoking is responsible for more than 480,000 deaths per year in the United States—480,000 human beings dead, every year, because of cigarette smoking. These people don't just die in their beds, unexpectedly and peacefully. Smoking increasingly clogs up your lungs until it eventually kills you. For years before they die most of these people struggle with their breathing, they go to the doctor, the doctor tells them to stop smoking, but they carry on. They make the same excuses you make: doctors don't know everything, they say everything gives you cancer these days, you've got to die of something, and of course the biggest and best excuse of them all: I will stop, yes, but just not today. Today isn't the right time. I'll stop tomorrow, next week, next month, after my birthday, after our next holiday, in fact any day at all as long as it isn't today!

How much power something holds over you is directly related to how much you want it. Imagine that there's a new burger joint opening, and it boasts the best burgers ever (don't they all?). As a promotion, they're giving away free burgers. You get one and try it, and it really is one fine burger, best you've ever had!

Then the promotion ends and the burgers start being sold at the normal price. Would you spend money on another one? That's going to depend on how much it costs, right? If they were being sold for a dollar, most people would have another one; after all, the burger was great and it was only a dollar! What about if it was $5? Probably the same. But what if those burgers were selling for $50? Or $500? Or $5,000? I mean, you're not going to spend $5,000 on a burger, are you? After all, it was good, but not *that* good!

The point is that how much you want something dictates how much power it has over you, or how much you are prepared to spend (or give up) for it. The higher your desire, the more you'll give up. You may think you'd never spend $500 on a burger, but what if you were starving and this was the only food available? If you were literally about to die from want of food? In that case, I think most of us would spend $500 on a burger; in fact, we'd most likely give anything and everything we owned for that burger. But on the other hand, if you'd just eaten so many burgers you could hardly move, you wouldn't accept another one even if they were being given away free, would you?

Your desire for something dictates how much power that something has over you. That something may have downsides, it may kill you, and a part of you may truly hate it, but whether that is enough to enable you to walk away from it depends on whether your dislike of it exceeds your desire for it. Your desire may be based on pleasure or necessity or a mix of the two; in other words, you may believe you enjoy smoking or you may believe that coping with life just isn't possible without it. For most people it's a mix of the two. But the fact is that however your desire for it is made up, the more desire you have for it, the more you will be prepared to give up for it, and the more power it will hold over you.

So, how do we get to the stage where nicotine holds so much power over us that we are literally willing to give up our very lives for it? And don't start thinking that you would never give up your life for it. This happens to nearly half a million Americans every single year.

Whether you smoke, vape, dip, or chew, the "pleasure" is all to do with nicotine. To fully understand the so-called pleasure of nicotine we need to understand how nicotine affects human beings, and to understand this we need to understand three things: the human brain, the nature of nicotine, and what happens when you put the two together.

The Human Brain

The human brain is arguably the most complicated and intricate organism on the planet. There is a lot we do not understand about it, how it works and how it reacts to stimulus, but what we do know is that it creates and excretes its own array of drugs, chemicals, and hormones. This is a phenomenally complicated and scarcely understood process, but what is clear is that the brain is constantly trying to maintain what is known as homeostasis, which is a delicate balance between all the drugs, hormones, and chemicals. The brain is constantly acting and reacting to keep this delicate balance in place. Any disruption to this balance will change how we feel; an imbalance can leave us feeling happy, sad, awake, or sleepy and has a direct impact on our mood, confidence, and alertness.

Nicotine

Nicotine is a powerful stimulant, which means it is something that increases the activity of the central nervous system and leaves us feeling more mentally alert and awake. It doesn't just have an effect on how we feel mentally, it also affects how we feel physically. Part of its simulating effect is that it increases our heart rate. The point with heart rate is that when you exercise, your heart rate increases to increase blood flow; your blood cells carry oxygen, energy, and nutrients to the muscles that need it. Everyone's heart has a maximum rate at which it can beat, and the higher it goes, the more your brain triggers the desire to sit down and rest. This is the mechanism by which your brain tries to stop you from overdoing physical activity. So the two main effects of nicotine are to make you feel more mentally alert, but to make you physically drained and tired.

When I was a smoker, I used to avoid physical activity, and I was all but incapable of running. I used to look on people who exercised as bizarre types prepared to undergo deep physical discomfort in order to live a few tiny years longer. What I never appreciated was that my deep aversion to exercise was due to my constantly elevated heart rate, which made physical activity difficult and unpleasant. Heart rate is measured in beats per minute (bpm), literally how many times your heart beats in a minute. I am now in my forties and my resting heart rate is consistently 42, and my maximum heart rate is around 195. So on average I have the potential for my heart rate to increase by around 153 beats. When I was a smoker in my twenties my heart rate after smoking a cigarette was around 80/90. This is high, and at the stage when your brain is starting to send the message that "This isn't quite right, you need to start slowing down now."

This is why I have more energy now, in my forties, than I did in my early twenties. As a smoker, those cigarettes made me feel constantly drained and lethargic, but I didn't ever associate that feeling with the cigarette. I just assumed that the feeling was how everyone felt and that only strange people felt it was necessary to exercise. What I didn't realize until I stopped was that when your heart rate returns to normal, exercise is not unpleasant and difficult, it is enjoyable and natural. Just as when your heart rate is high you want to sit down and rest, so when your heart rate starts to lower you actually want to get out, to get some ground under your feet, and to get out into the world.

You may smoke or vape and consider yourself to be fit and strong, but the simple fact is that you will not be as fit or as strong or as energetic as you would be without having nicotine accelerating your heart rate.

ENGAGEMENT POINT

If you are still smoking, concentrate on identifying this feeling of being drained and feeling lethargic. Before you smoke, move around a little bit, take a walk or even (if you can) a little jog. Move your arms and legs around, see how heavy they feel and see how much effort it is to move them. If there's something heavy nearby, pick it up and see how heavy it feels. The sit down and smoke your cigarette. Smoke it quickly and as soon as you finish it, jump up and try to do those activities over again and see how much harder they are, and how much more effort you have to put in with the elevated heart rate caused by the nicotine.

Nicotine and the Brain Combined

In the section above we talk a little about how nicotine affects human beings, but we only talk about the immediate effect—that of creating chemical stimulation. However, this effect is not constant. The human brain is not a passive lump of putty that just sits there, doing its own thing, regardless of any external stimuli. Your brain is reactive; it reacts to the world around it and it reacts to any external drugs you consume. So how does it do this?

In respect to any drugs you consume (like nicotine), the brain immediately recognizes that homeostasis—the delicate internal chemical balance—has been upset and it takes steps to redress the balance. How it does this is complicated and not fully understood, but essentially it attempts to counter the overstimulation.

Think about a set of weighing scales with, on the one hand, stimulants, and on the other side, depressants. Your brain is constantly seeking to keep these scales in balance because when they are in balance you feel positive, buoyant, and competent. That is not to say that you are constantly happy because life consists of ups and downs, and the downs always come along to test us, but unless the problems are serious, you feel able to deal with them without them derailing you too much.

So we have a set of scales that are fairly equally balanced. We smoke, or we vape or chew or dip, and suddenly the stimulant side of the scales shoots up. Your brain tries to redress this balance by increasing the depressant side of the scales. As mentioned, the exact mechanism the brain uses to do this is complicated and not fully understood, but it is likely that it increases the output of its own naturally occurring depressants, becomes less reactive to existing stimulants, and removes any existing stimulants far sooner than it would otherwise.

The problem then, of course, is that the nicotine is removed from your system, or to go back to the weighing scale analogy, the weight starts to come off the stimulant side. This then causes another imbalance, this time the other way.

It can be easier to picture this using the following very simple graphs.

This first graph illustrates how we are naturally, without any external drugs. As you can see, the stimulants and depressants are roughly equal.

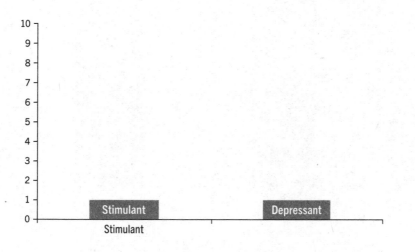

This second graph is what happens when we take a dose of nicotine. As you can see, the stimulant side of things increases dramatically.

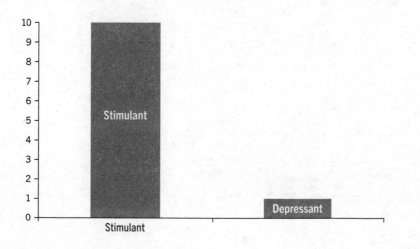

The third graph below shows what happens when the brain has taken steps to counter the overstimulation. As you can see, it has pushed up the depressant side of things in an attempt to rebalance the imbalance caused by the dose of nicotine.

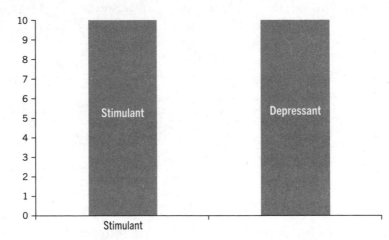

The nicotine then wears off, leaving a chemical imbalance the other way. This is seen in the graph below.

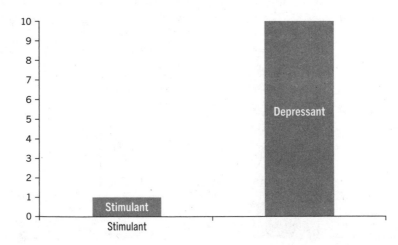

This final graph shows the nicotine "withdrawal" phase. Withdrawal is essentially an unpleasant feeling caused when the effects of a drug have worn off, and it is a feeling that can most quickly be relieved by another dose of the same drug; after all, the quickest way to rectify this imbalance is to take another dose of nicotine, which brings the stimulant level back up and redresses the chemical imbalance that has been caused by the previous cigarette.

When we are in the nicotine withdrawal phase we may feel slightly groggy, not really with it, woolly-headed. However, by far the most important effect from the perspective of understanding nicotine's addictive qualities is that it leaves us feeling slightly less able to cope with things. That chemical imbalance leaves us feeling out of sorts and less well equipped to deal with life. It amounts to having less mental resilience, so that smaller and smaller problems are able to derail us, and even leave us frozen, like a rabbit in the headlights of an oncoming vehicle. Instead of being able to see solutions to problems, problems start to overwhelm us, and as the mental grogginess makes it hard for us to see solutions, it also makes it hard for us to take the necessary action to make those solutions happen. In short, we become mentally weaker, more frail, slightly confused, and unable to take clear, decisive action to rectify things and keep our lives on track. We end up like a tired toddler, ready to throw our toys out of the stroller at the slightest provocation.

Of course, the quickest way to relieve this withdrawal and to rebalance the brain is to take another dose of the drug. In doing so, we redress the imbalance by pushing up the stimulant side of the scales and so create a much closer balance between stimulants and depressants. This is what you can see in the graph on the following page.

This is, in essence, the pleasure of smoking, vaping, dipping, or chewing. This is the crux of any form of nicotine addiction. This is what you get in return for the lethargy, the heaviness, the shortened life span, the

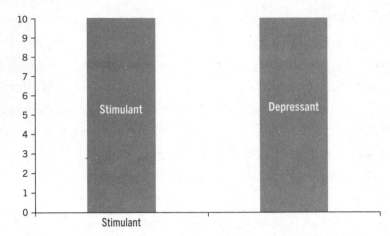

cost, the health risks. This is where the feeling of confidence, happiness, and satisfaction comes from. It comes from relieving the withdrawal that has been caused by the previous dose of nicotine.

ENGAGEMENT POINT

When you take your next dose of nicotine, try to identify all of these feelings; how you feel before, during, and after you get that nicotine into your bloodstream. Try to start really analyzing how it makes you feel and what it actually does for you. Isn't it the case that you feel on edge and out of sorts when you aren't smoking, then no longer on edge and out of sorts when you smoke? Start watching smokers, particularly when they aren't able to smoke. Are they fiddling with things, constantly on edge, unrelaxed, and nervous? Look at non-smokers. Do they look eternally anxious and unsatisfied because they aren't smoking? Or do they look relaxed and content without a cigarette?

Smokers believe that smoking relaxes them and gives them confidence. This is such a basic tenet of smoking that smokers rarely even question it. But if I give you $100, you're $100 better off, right? That's a no-brainer. In fact, you're going to be happy to have me around all the time if I keep doing it! But what if you find out that I'm stealing money directly out of your bank account, and for every $100 I give you I've first stolen $200 from you? This is not only nicotine, but drug addiction generally: you get nothing other than the partial return of something already lost.

Knowledge and understanding are everything. When you know better, you do better.

ENGAGEMENT POINT

Start to ask yourself exactly what you are achieving when you smoke, because if smoking doesn't actually give you anything at all, if it just takes away and then partially restores, then the benefits of smoking— the supposed gain you achieve for all the expense and the health risks— is total illusion. Also, start to consider how much time you spend thinking about smoking. As soon as you put a cigarette out, the nicotine starts to leave your system, and that delicate chemical balance that leaves you feeling confident and resilient starts to unravel, and you feel increasingly out of sorts.

Go back to your list of benefits of smoking. Think about the physiological process at play, that as the nicotine starts to wear off, you feel slightly strange and out or sorts. It a very elusive feeling and can be hard to pinpoint, but it is there and has been there throughout your smoking life. In many ways it's not very noticeable, but it manifests itself in a feeling of not being quite able to deal with things so easily. Think about how it feels to relieve that feeling, to go from feeling "off" and unhappy to going back to your usual confident and positive self. You may not think of yourself as being confident and positive, and compared to others you may not be, but the fact is that you are more positive and confident without the nicotine withdrawal than with it.

Think carefully about the pleasure you feel from being able to change your mental state as you move out of withdrawal. Look at your list of benefits. Do you enjoy smoking? Are certain situations improved by it? Can you think of any situation that wouldn't be improved by changing your mood and outlook from out of sorts and groggy to positive and confident? If you have listed enjoyment, can you see where the pleasure is? And that it is a false pleasure? It is not a gain, but it is a way to restore something that has previously been taken from you.

Perhaps on your list of benefits you have written that smoking a cigarette gives you time to yourself to reflect. Ask yourself why you can't have that without a cigarette. Even the most extroverted of people need some time alone, and the less extroverted you are the more time alone you need. Most lifestyles these days require constant interaction with others (either work or family) and some time alone can be extremely pleasant. Why can't you enjoy this time without a cigarette? After all, people who don't smoke manage this all the time.

Think about these benefits of smoking. Is smoking actually adding any pleasure? Or is it just removing an aggravation that it caused in the first place? Isn't it the case that, far from adding enjoyment, the reality is that you can't enjoy the situation without a cigarette? Are non-smokers incapable of relaxing, having some time out, socializing, and so forth because they don't smoke? Or is the reality that non-smokers know how to enjoy all those things without having to smoke?

4.

Vaping:
Making Nicotine Trendy Again

Have you ever heard of Mrs. Winslow's Soothing Syrup? It was a concoction that claimed to quiet restless children and babies, particularly while teething. If you have children you will know that, for most, the more difficult part of early childhood, insofar as parents are concerned, is the lack of sleep. Very few babies sleep through the night; they wake up regularly for feeding, dirty diapers that need changing, or just because they've had enough sleep and decided that now just feels like the right time to wake up and start screaming. They are usually just about at the stage of sleeping through the night (much to the relief of the parents) when they start teething and so are up all night again crying from their aching gums.

Something that can calm a baby down and send them off to sleep is pretty priceless, so, when it was introduced in 1845, the use of Mrs. Winslow's Soothing Syrup became widespread.

What was in this miraculous formula that helped babies sleep so soundly? In fact it contained morphine. Each dose of Mrs. Winslow's Soothing Syrup contained a hefty dose of morphine. So yes, it did indeed quiet restless babies and it also alleviated teething pain, but it also killed them. It was eventually withdrawn from sale in 1930.

The fact is that years ago drugs weren't seen in the same way that they are now. You could go into a pharmacy and buy morphine, heroin, and cocaine the same way that today you can buy acetaminophen and heartburn relievers. Far less was understood about the addictive nature of these drugs and they were evaluated only on their immediate effect. So the baby's been crying all night and you're exhausted. No problem. Give the baby some morphine to help it go to sleep, and take some cocaine or methamphetamine as a pick-me-up.

Drugs such as these were often sold as "tonics," and that is exactly how they were perceived—as something that is full of things that are healthy and good for you, so when you take it you feel better. Compared to today, very little was understood about drugs (and vitamins) and what could harm you. If you took something and it made you feel better, it was generally considered to be good. This didn't just apply to drugs such as morphine and cocaine, but also to smoking and nicotine. At the turn of the twentieth century, many, many more people smoked, people drank more, and taking other drugs was perfectly normal. Sherlock Holmes, Sir Arthur Conan Doyle's famous detective who first appeared in print in the 1880s, used to drink, smoke, and take cocaine.

Because these substances were enjoyed and even celebrated, a whole culture grew up around them. In 1916, the famous store Harrods in London sold a kit described as "A Welcome Present for Friends at the Front" (soldiers fighting in World War I) containing cocaine, morphine, syringes, and needles. Cut glass ashtrays, cigarette lighters, and cigarette cases were in vogue as gifts. As our view of these drugs has turned from seeing them as something healthy and beneficial to destructive and fatal, so the culture of acceptability that surrounded them has deteriorated. Cigarette cases aren't really popular anymore, and it is unusual to give someone a lighter for one of those coming-of-age birthdays, like turning twenty-one. At least on the whole it has. There is, of course, one notable exception: vaping.

Vaping almost turns the entire phenomenon of the unacceptability of addiction on its head. All other forms of drug addiction are becoming less and less acceptable, and are being pushed more and more to the periphery. Smoking is banned in more and more places; no longer do you walk into a bar to find the air thick with smoke. Smokers are having to go outside to smoke, to leave the main group, have their quick fix, and return.

The point of smoking or vaping is to get nicotine inside your body. That really is the crux of it. The hype that I refer to is all the additional peripherals, the way we dress up a rather unpleasant core with a veneer to give it acceptability. With smoking it was the cigarette cases, the polished metal lighters, the attractive ashtrays, smoking jackets, and smoking rooms. With heroin addiction it was the glass syringes in leather cases. A lot of these things are totally outmoded now, even alien. Imagine for example walking into Walmart and seeing a nice leather case containing syringes "for your mainling pleasure."

The hype surrounding cigarette addiction is being left behind, but the trends surrounding vaping, to a large degree, are going the other way. You can now spend hundreds of dollars on limited-edition handcrafted vaping devices made by skilled engineers, and some of the groups you need to be in to get access to these require two other people to vouch for you. There are trade fairs, three-hundred-dollar cases made of wood, and vape celebrities (one of whom has clocked up almost 200,000,000 YouTube views). These vape celebrities don't just do reviews, but also give tutorials and offer anti-regulation rhetoric.

Keeping in mind what vaping is—nicotine addiction, pure and simple— the culture that has built up around it is extraordinary, particularly so when you consider that is was originally developed as a quitting aid that has now developed into a subgenre of nicotine addiction in its own right. One of the reasons for this, of course, is that it is a tech product in a society that is obsessed with technology. But if vaping and smoking are both about addiction to nicotine, why can it be so hard for some people to transition from the one to the other?

One of the reasons is that inhaling cigarette smoke does feel very different from inhaling vapor. Later in the book we cover the issue of the harmfulness of vaping, but for now what you need to be aware of is that cigarette smoke contains a lot of things other than just nicotine. When you breathe it in, it feels very heavy and solid, whereas vaping is quite the opposite. In fact, for people who are used to smoking, vaping feels like nothing at all, it's almost like breathing ordinary air (albeit with the flavor of Hubba Bubba bubble gum or cherry cola or "raspberry and sarsaparilla white chocolate muffin" or whatever weird flavor is added to it).

Because we associate the relieving of the withdrawal with that feeling of inhaling smoke, any change to that feeling immediately feels wrong, so our knee-jerk reaction is to reject it. But if you persevere, your brain very quickly learns to link this new, slightly lighter sensation with the relieving of the withdrawal—it just takes some time for your brain to relearn the sensations related to it.

ENGAGEMENT POINT

If you vape, think about what you actually enjoy about vaping. It really comes down to three things: taste, the sensation of the vapor going into your lungs, and the feeling you get when the nicotine hits your bloodstream. Think about what the main pull is, what the great pleasure in it is for you.

5.

Is Smoking a Habit?

A lot of people think of smoking as a habit. This may not seem a like a particularly important point, but it is one that we need to dissect and analyze and understand fully in our conscious mind, because it has implications beyond being just an academic point. After all, if smoking *is* just a habit, then there is a very important conclusion that we can draw, specifically that we can cut down or reduce our intake. After all, we can and do change our habits. I am in the habit of going out cycling each day during the week, but on the weekend I tend not to cycle because that is time I spend with my family. I slip from the one habit to the other with no effort at all. I cycle on the weekdays, and don't cycle on the weekend.

Vacations are another example. When I'm on vacation, my habit is to eat breakfast, then lie around outside in my swimsuit. A perfectly natural and understandable habit to get into. But I don't then follow that habit when I am home. On a normal working day in mid-January you won't find me eating breakfast, then changing into my swimsuit to lie in my garden in subzero temperatures while my boss wonders why on earth I'm not at my desk working.

So, if smoking is a habit, we should be able to get into the habit of smoking less, or smoking on the weekend, or when we go out with friends. In other words, we should be able to cut back, and after a few days when we get into the habit of smoking less, it will be easy and natural for us to smoke this reduced amount. But what is a habit? And is smoking really even a habit?

A habit is just a routine of behavior that one voluntarily repeats on a regular basis because it has certain benefits, like lying around outside after breakfast, or cycling on certain days and not on others.

Now, let's compare that with addiction, and nicotine addiction in particular. Remember, when you take a dose of nicotine it soon wears off, leaving an unpleasant, insecure feeling and another dose of nicotine is needed to replace it. Relieving this unpleasant feeling provides the only real pleasure in smoking.

When you have your very first cigarette, your body and brain have never encountered nicotine before. It's a new experience and your system has no experience of how to counter its stimulating effects. Quickly, your brain becomes proficient at countering and incorporating the effect of the nicotine with the result that in a very short space of time you suffer from full nicotine withdrawal. Withdrawal starts to kick in as soon as the last breath of smoke (or vapor) has left your lungs.

However, addiction isn't just physical, it is also mental. In the early stages of our smoking career, not only is the withdrawal less severe, but we are less attuned to it. As the nicotine wears off you may feel slightly insecure, slightly out of sorts, slightly less mentally resilient and confident than you ordinarily would. But this is a vague feeling, and it is very hard to pin down. There are lots of times in your life when you may have a similar feeling, for example, if you are about to do something you are nervous about, such as attend a meeting or give a presentation or take a test. So we have this vague, unpleasant feeling, but at this early stage we may not even be consciously aware of it. Also, it would never dawn on either our conscious or subconscious mind to reach for a cigarette to re-lieve it.

This is the "take it or leave it" stage of drug addiction. We do suffer from the withdrawal, but we don't immediately think of smoking a ciga-rette to relieve it.

Over time, and with regular doses of the drug, both our conscious and subconscious mind learn an important lesson that forms the back-bone of addiction: that another dose of the drug in question will relieve that unpleasant feeling we get when the previous dose wears off.

This key point—that another dose of the drug in question will relieve that unpleasant feeling we get when the previous dose wears off—is learned. We learn that lesson, and the lesson is emphasized and made stronger with every subsequent dose of nicotine that we take.

The point is that once we've learned this lesson, it can never be un-learned. After all, it's true; another dose of nicotine *does* relieve the un-pleasant feeling that we get when the previous dose starts to wear off. It's not something we can then forget, or unlearn. It is with us for life.

Imagine if you'd never encountered the concepts of math before. I could quite easily teach you the basic concept of numbering, and I could teach you why two plus two equals four. That would be a fairly easy task. But, what I could never do would be to then *unteach* that lesson to you and make you forget the concepts involved. You'll always know that two plus two equals four.

So, when you learn the lesson about the cycle of nicotine on both a conscious and subconscious level, whenever you experience the with-drawal, your brain (either the conscious part of the subconscious part or even both parts) will trigger the thought that you need to reach for a ciga-rette to relieve that uncomfortable feeling.

This process continues as we become more and more attuned to the withdrawal. In our early smoking career, the withdrawal will have to be-come quite significant for it to come to our attention, but as we learn through dose after dose that a further dose will relieve the withdrawal, we become increasingly attuned to the withdrawal and we start to notice it at an earlier and earlier stage. And so, the period between each dose of nicotine tends to reduce as time goes by.

Of course, the tendency to increase one's intake varies from individual to individual. Most people have constraints on when they can smoke, such as a work environment where they can only smoke at certain times during the day. Others are so worried about their smoking that they keep strictly to a certain level and are too afraid to increase it. Others may not be able to afford to smoke more than they do. Some may only smoke at social occasions or when they drink, and they may have a strong mental barrier in place against smoking on any other occasion. All these factors and more may mean that some people are able to maintain their current intake at a certain level for many years, even for their whole lives, but the point is that this is very unusual and certainly not the natural tendency. The natural tendency, for anyone, is to feel good, not bad. We don't want to feel insecure and out of sorts, we want to feel relaxed and confident. In other words, we want to alleviate the withdrawal instead of suffer it. We want to take the drug instead of go without it. Of course there is the cost, the health fears, the restrictions on when and where we are allowed to smoke, and many other factors that cause us to limit or restrict our intake, that stop us from chain-smoking. These apply to everyone to a greater or lesser degree, but the point is that we do not want to feel groggy, out of sorts, and unable to cope. We want to feel calm, in control, and confident. And we don't want to wait five or ten or twenty minutes to feel good, we want to feel that way NOW! So although most people don't chain-smoke, it is the theoretical natural tendency. We want to relieve the withdrawal, not suffer it.

When we have this simple understanding in place we can draw a few important conclusions about our smoking.

1. When we started smoking we may very well have gone through a stage where we genuinely could take it or leave it. We may have gone whole days or weeks without smoking. We may have started off only smoking on certain occasions (like when we were drinking or out with friends). However, this is a one-off stage. It is not one that you can ever return to.

2. Taking a drug is not a habit, it is addiction. A habit is repeating a certain behavior because it is beneficial. Addiction is being compelled to take a poison in order to alleviate an unpleasant feeling. You may get used to relieving your withdrawal on certain occasions (like getting into your car) or at certain times of the day (like when you wake up), but the relieving of the withdrawal is not habit, but necessity.

In other words, smoking is like a one-way street. You can't backtrack. You can't go back to an earlier stage when you smoked less or smoked only in certain situations. You may be able to cut back on your intake by constantly having to resist temptation, but you will not be able to return to that earlier stage when it felt normal or natural to smoke at that level. If you smoke twenty a day now, and you want to go back to just smoking two or three a day, or just smoking on the weekend when you go out drinking, you may be able to force yourself to do this for limited time periods, but it will never feel natural to do so, and you won't ever be happy doing it. You will never get into the so-called habit of only smoking on those occasions, because as soon as the nicotine starts to leave your body the withdrawal kicks in, and as soon as it does so and as soon and you notice it (either consciously or subconsciously) you will want a cigarette. You may be able to resist having one, you may even be able to distract yourself from thinking about it, but it will always mean effort and a battle.

ENGAGEMENT POINT

Think about some of your habitual behaviors, and think about how they change as your situation changes. Do you get up later on a working day than a nonworking day? Do you eat meals at different times? Do your daily habits change if you are on vacation? How difficult is it to change these habits? Do you ever find yourself on vacation, miserable and anxious because you're finding it desperately hard to get out of the "habit" of getting up at 6 a.m. to go to work?

Think about some of your so-called habits that are hard to break or cut down. How many of these involve drugs (remembering of course that nicotine, caffeine, and alcohol are drugs; just because a drug is legal and widely available does not mean that it is not a drug)?

You may think about a certain behavior, like biting your nails, that does not involve a drug and yet is hard to stop doing. A lot of nail biters also consume nicotine or caffeine on a regular basis. Many people find that the habit of nail biting is in fact much easier to stop when they quit nicotine. Remember, nicotine is a stimulant that leaves us feeling uptight, and the withdrawal leaves us feeling a bit anxious. Both of these make us feel restless and make us want to be constantly doing something with our hands. Nail biting is therefore something that comes very naturally to nicotine addicts. In fact, nail biting isn't just a habit anyway—animals gnaw their nails (or claws) to both clean them and to stop them from getting too long. It's not something we do repeatedly because it is beneficial to do so, it is something we are compelled to do by a primitive instinct.

Start to watch smokers, vapers, and dippers and compare them to non-smokers, non-vapers, and non-dippers. Which of these people look more relaxed generally? Which seem to be more on edge, constantly moving around, constantly having to fiddle with things or bite their nails?

6.

The Human Experience

Life is generally supposed to be enjoyable. Yes, it has its difficult parts, but there should always be more joy than pain. Human beings are incredibly resilient, you only have to look back over history to see untold numbers of stories of people, everyday ordinary people, going through hell and coming out the other side to live happy, productive lives. Stories of people who went through the Holocaust, spent years in a concentration camp, lost all their friends and their family, yet still survived and found love and happiness. It never ceases to amaze and astound me to realize what people can go through when they have to.

Most of us are lucky enough that we never have to go through anything like the Holocaust. You may think that you simply wouldn't be able to cope if something like that happened to you, but actually, when push comes to shove, people can cope through extraordinary challenges better than they may think. After all, we do what we need to do to survive.

Even though most of us will, hopefully, never experience something as horrific as the Holocaust, we do all have bad days, and some days are worse than others. How much we are able to cope with is really down to how mentally resilient we are. Let me explain further.

Imagine that problems in life come on a scale of 1 to 10, with 1 being the most minor problems, and 10 being the most extreme. So a 1 might be a bill to pay when you have the money to pay it. So you've got the money, but you still need to go online to pay it, or send off a check. It's not a major thing, an irritant more than anything, but still something you could do without.

A 3 or 4 might be a problem like your internet acting up, so you can't do your work or watch that TV show you were looking forward to, and you know you're going to end up waiting the best part of forty minutes on hold to your broadband provider. They agree to send out a technician, but the next available slot is in three weeks' time, and it's fifty-fifty whether they actually arrive on the day at all, and even if they do there's a slim to nonexistent chance of them actually being able to fix it anyway.

Problems ranked a 7 or 8 might be the loss of a job, shortage of money, health issues, relationship breakups, and the like. The 9s and 10s are death or serious injury of a loved one. Obviously, this scale will look different for different people, but you get the idea.

So, as you get up the scale to the higher numbers, the problems not only get more serious but they also become rarer. The 1s and 2s are going to be hitting you all the time: the car needs filling up with gas, you need to pop out for some milk, the housework needs doing, and so on. A 9 or 10 problem will hit you, and they hit everyone, but hopefully only a few times over your entire life.

The amount of mental resilience you have is essentially measurable by the level of problem you are able to deal with without becoming de-railed. Are you someone who can go through life batting away everything up to a 7 or 8 without breaking stride? Or do you find yourself struggling with the 4s and 5s?

Of course, different people have different levels of mental resilience.

But even the same person does not have a constant level—it will fluctuate over time and in different situations. Part of this is dictated by our physical state. If we are feeling well, physically and mentally, our mental resilience goes up. And if we aren't feeling well, it goes down. This is just good common sense, if you think about it. If a living creature is feeling good and on top of its game, it needs to get out there—to find food, to find a mate, to find a good water source, to find a good territory to live in. Physical health brings with it a corresponding feeling of being able to cope, a feeling even of being adventurous, brave, carefree. Compare this to when you don't feel well, if you have the flu or food poisoning. All you want to do is curl up in a bed and be left alone. If you have something you have to do, such as look after the kids, or go to work, or help someone out, you can almost feel panicked. You don't feel confident or adventurous and you certainly don't feel like getting out into the world and living life. You feel tired and vulnerable and weak and in need of comfort. If you are feeling well and healthy you might be able to deal with the 5s and 6s, no problem, but when you aren't well you might not even be able to face the 1s. After all, who goes online to pay a non-urgent bill when they're feeling awful with the flu?

This is just nature's way; a healthy animal needs to be out there making the best of its opportunities, a sick or injured animal needs to find somewhere safe to hide and recover. It shouldn't be out in the big wide world where it might have to fight (or run) for its life.

So what does all this have to do with smoking? Well, the fact of the matter is that to be at your most resilient mentally, you need to be physically well and you need that delicate chemical balance in your mind, homeostasis, to be working at its best. Smoking does two things. First, it interrupts homeostasis, leaving you less mentally resilient than you ought to be. Second, it erodes your fitness and health generally, which further decreases your ability to cope with life.

Imagine a causeway across a marsh. For those not familiar with a causeway, it's a raised path or road that provides a way of crossing otherwise impassable or difficult to negotiate land. Imagine you're walking across this causeway, but there's a crosswind. This crosswind never quite disappears, but it does get stronger and weaker as the weather changes. Sometimes it's almost unnoticeable, other times it gets stronger and can make you stagger a bit, on rare occasions it can blow you right over. It's OK, though, because this causeway was built by people who knew about the wind, and it was designed with the wind in mind. It's wide. Good and wide. So even the strongest wind, the unexpected one that seems to come out of nowhere when you're least expecting it and throws you right onto your face, doesn't knock you off the causeway and into the marsh. You have a good ten feet of causeway on each side of you, so although you may get the odd time when you stagger off course, and on rare occasions go right off your feet and end up face-first in the dirt, you don't end up going over the side of the causeway into the marsh. You may be blown a bit off course and you may end up on your face, but you can pick yourself up, dust yourself off, and keep walking, and even though you might end up a bit bruised and bloody from your fall, as soon as you get up and start walking again your body starts healing from the knock you took.

If that journey across the causeway is your journey through life, and the crosswind is all the trials and tribulations that every human being on the planet has to put up with to one degree or another, the width of that causeway is your mental resilience. The times you get ill, that causeway gets narrower and narrower, until even the smaller winds can blow you off the side.

Because drugs interfere with the delicate chemical balance of our brains, they seek to counter the effect a drug has on us. When the drug wears off there is another imbalance in the brain, one that needs another dose of the drug to redress it. A drug may make you feel more alert or more relaxed, but as time goes on you end up taking that drug just to feel normal. With drugs, you get nothing for free, and I'm not talking about the financial costs, I'm talking purely in terms of how they make you feel. The first dose of nicotine may make you feel more alert and focused, but you are not designed to feel that alert and focused all the time. So your brain recalibrates; it becomes less alert and less focused to counter the effects of the nicotine. Without the nicotine you feel slightly disoriented and out of sorts. You then take the nicotine and get back to your usual confident and resilient self (whatever that level may ordinarily be).

This is just the chemical effect of the drug on your mental state. As we've already covered, nicotine also has an effect on your fitness generally by increasing your heart rate. As your heart rate increases you feel more lethargic, less energetic, more inclined to want to sit down and rest. This is the complete opposite of feeling energetic and wanting to get out there and seize the day.

There is, in addition to this, the psychological effect of smoking. Most people know in their heart of hearts that smoking isn't doing them any favors, that they are spending a lot of money on something that is killing them, and that they are doing this not through genuine choice but because they are in the grip of something that they don't understand. Because they believe they can't stop, they try to bury these thoughts. Most of the time we are able to do this and put these thoughts out of our minds, but they will still be there, weighing us down even as we try to ignore them.

So let's say that your normal mental resilience gives you a nice wide causeway of twenty feet. Wide enough to give you a good bit of leeway. Wide enough so that even the strong winds aren't going to send you over the edge. When you start smoking you introduce three things that affect the width of that causeway: the interference with your brain's chemistry, the impact on your heart rate and physical health generally, and those never-ending worries that we do our best to ignore.

Obviously, the exact effect of these will vary from individual to individual, and will also affect them differently at different stages of their lives. Some people may be very good at conning themselves into thinking that the very real health risks of smoking won't affect them in the same way they affect other people.

It's also the case, of course, that if you are in your twenties, the thought of dying in your fifties instead of your eighties is probably easier to ignore. But if you're in your fifties and your doctor is already telling you that you are in imminent danger of a heart attack, the health issues are going to be far harder to close your mind to.

There will be a variation in how much the above points affect you, but let's assume for the moment that these work to knock off, say, four feet of width from your causeway, leaving you sixteen feet. Still fairly wide, right? But the effect of nicotine on your heart and energy levels is huge and immediate. It takes you from the default state of being energetic and enthusiastic (and I emphasize that this is a default state; no one, be they smoker or non-smoker, is happy all the time) to feeling heavy and lackluster. This is going to knock eight feet off, leaving you around eight feet to play with.

Then we factor in the actual chemical effects on the brain. The withdrawal is a subtle feeling, many people live their whole lives without every really identifying it and appreciating that it's there. It's vague and hard to put your finger on, but it isn't pleasant. It's a feeling, as we've learned, of being slightly woolly-headed, being slightly out of focus with life, of feeling less confident and less able to cope with life.

So with the eight feet you have left, you are going to swing from maybe having around three feet when the withdrawal is at its most severe, and around eight feet when you're relieving it.

A twenty-foot causeway is great—it gives you all the space you need to walk that path without fear, even in the strongest of winds. That's you, where your fitness and heart rate is where it ought to be, and your brain chemistry where it ought to be. Confident, happy, enthusiastic. Sure, we're all different, and some people are going to have a default state that is more confident than others, but the fact is, *you are at your personal best.* This is the key. Whatever your starting point, you are at your best.

So twenty feet is great, but three feet isn't. Three feet is scary. At three feet, much smaller things are going to totally derail you. If that causeway is only three feet wide, you'll do anything to increase it by a few feet. You become *desperate.* And that is really where addiction ends up. Imagine you're on a three-foot-wide causeway and the strong winds start. You'd be in a panic, you'd do anything to widen that causeway and that is why, when smokers do get to the stage where the doctor tells them they'll die if they don't quit, they still can't do so. Because when the big winds start we become even more desperate to widen that causeway. We want any bit of comfort we can lay our hands on.

And this is the real irony and horror of nicotine addiction. Even when taking the drug, even when we have all the comfort and confidence we get from a cigarette at its very highest, we are far, far worse off than someone who has never taken it. We go through so much, we give up so much: money, health, peace of mind, confidence, energy, in essence we give up our quality of life, and all so we can feel slightly more like we'd feel had we never taken that first experimental dose. But the more we give up, the more insecure and disoriented we feel, the more the nicotine robs us of our health, confidence, and self-respect, the more desperately we need it; the more desperate we are to claw back every precious inch of that ever-shrinking causeway by which we negotiate our journey through life.

If you are young and consider yourself to be otherwise healthy, it may seem alien and even impossible to reach the stage where the doctor tells you that you're going to die of smoking unless you quit, yet you continue to smoke anyway. But think about the unpleasant feeling you get when the nicotine wears off. Think about how important it is to you to keep relieving it, how it's so very, very easy to have just one more cigarette and to put off quitting until tomorrow. Imagine how much harder it will be when that causeway is so narrow you can scarcely balance on it even when the wind is very light, how much more desperate you will be to widen that causeway by even just a few inches.

This is also why, with addiction, it's *never* the right time to quit. In the early days we still believe we enjoy it, and the physical and mental drag hasn't yet reached full force. So we have more reasons to smoke and fewer reasons to stop. But as time goes by, although we may start to hate it more and more, we find it increasingly difficult to stop. In the early days we don't have the reason to stop, and in the later days we don't have the ability.

What you need to take away from this chapter is the knowledge that your body is incredibly strong, both physically and mentally. Sure, you may not be as strong as other people, but equally there are a lot of other people who are not as strong as you. The key point here is not where you fall on the scale, but *that you are at your best, physically and mentally, when you aren't smoking.*

ENGAGEMENT POINT

A lot of people who smoke or vape or dip regularly end up thinking of themselves as weak or deficient in some way. They feel like they need their drug in some way to deal with life and that they are incomplete without it. As we've covered here, this isn't the case at all, and it is just the drug that makes them feel this way. Think back to the time before you started smoking. Were you weak or deficient then? Can you think of occasions where you excelled in a sport (it doesn't have to be formal team sports, it could just be that you used to enjoy walking or swimming or cycling). Were there times when you "led the pack" at school? Spend a bit of time thinking back to the time before you started smoking and what you were really like then, in terms of physical activity and confidence.

7.

Are We Really Smoking for the Taste?

Years ago, a lot of people believed they smoked for the taste. But the appeal of smoking is more complex than that. Smoking is an experience made up of a mix of sensations and feelings all combined together, and most people never go through the process of breaking this experience down into its constituent parts and analyzing each of them. Let's do that now.

When we smoke, there is the feel of having something in our hands, the feel of it in our mouth, the taste of the smoke in our mouths, the feeling of breathing that smoke into our lungs, then the feeling of the nicotine as the drug is absorbed through our lungs and into our bloodstream, and is pumped around our bodies and in particular to our brain.

Most of these sensations are either banal or unpleasant. The feel of the cigarette or vape in our hands is neither positive nor negative; it is just a thing. The taste of smoke in our mouths and the feeling of it as we breathe it into our lungs is actively unpleasant. The only sensation that has any "pleasure" to it is when the nicotine hits our bloodstream and we can feel the effect of it. Because that sensation feels pleasant, we start to associate all of the other sensations with that pleasure because we experience them all together; it is one effect for us.

Some people genuinely believe that they enjoy the feel of the smoke going into their lungs. But when most people first smoke or vape, they cough. This is the body's natural reaction: smoke is damaging to our lungs, so the body reacts by trying to forcefully expel it as soon as possible, by coughing. However, almost immediately after that, your body senses a change, it feels different. After a few puffs your body and brain start to associate the sensation of inhaling smoke with the nicotine hitting your bloodstream, which also replaces the nicotine that is rapidly leaving your system. Your brain is fooled into thinking that something that is damaging—breathing in smoke or vapor containing nicotine—is actually beneficial.

The same principle applies to the taste. The taste of smoking is just the taste of burnt leaves. It's nothing remotely pleasant. The only reason people are fooled into thinking that the taste is pleasant is because they associate it with the experience of putting nicotine into their bloodstreams, which ends the feeling of the withdrawal.

Things can be slightly more complicated with vaping and dipping. Think of the point of smoking as getting the drug into your bloodstream, but it's an extremely damaging poison so your body has certain mechanisms to keep it out of your system. One is taste and one is coughing. Your brain needs to reinterpret both the taste and the sensation of inhaling smoke before smoking or inhaling can be bearable.

With vaping, the mechanism is different, it's only the inhalation that needs to be overcome because the vapor contains additional chemicals to give it a more palatable flavor, hence the flavoring of cherry, white chocolate, gummy bears, and so forth. Also because there are far fewer chemicals and particles in vapor than in tobacco smoke, breathing it into the lungs tends to be far less offensive, so generally it is easier to become addicted to vaping than smoking. Some people believe they vape for the taste, in the same way people will sometimes say that they smoke for the taste. If this were true, then quitting would be very simple; you would just need to switch to a nicotine-free vape or cigarette. But for most people, nicotine-free varieties just don't seem to "taste" the same. The real issue here is not taste but perception.

In this book we've broken down smoking and vaping into its constituent parts so that we can fully evaluate and understand it. But that's not how people experience it. People don't light up a cigarette and think about the withdrawal, the increased heart rate, the taste, the effect on their lungs, and so forth. All they experience is the momentary act of smoking or vaping. They experience all the different aspects of it at once and so their impression is that overall they "enjoy" it.

What they ascribe to taste is actually the whole experience of smoking, including the relieving of the withdrawal. Smokers and vapers often ascribe their enjoyment specifically to taste because it can be the most noticeable of all the sensations that together make up our experience of smoking or vaping.

Dip is slightly different; again there are chemicals added to make the flavor more palatable (most commonly wintergreen) but of course with dip, you don't inhale it. With dip, the equivalent of inhaling is the burning gums. Again, like inhaling smoke, it's the feeling of your body being damaged, but the effect of the drug causes your brain to reinterpret this feeling as a good thing.

ENGAGEMENT POINT

Think about the concept of an "acquired taste." This is essentially when we try something, don't like it, but with repeated exposure to it "learn" to enjoy it.

Taste is a chemical reaction wherein sensors in your mouth (mainly on your tongue) react chemically with what is in your mouth. This is an objective chemical reaction and cannot change with age or time. The flavor (that is, the actual chemical reaction) does not change, the only part that can change is how your brain interprets that flavor. The flavor remains the same but your brain reassesses your reaction to it based on its effect. If you consume something unpalatable but it assuages your hunger and doesn't make you ill, eventually you will believe that you enjoy it. Think about how this applies to smoking, vaping, and dipping.

The Impact

’ve mentioned previously how cigarette smoking is responsible for more than 480,000 deaths per year in the United States. That's an awful lot of deaths. But in many ways these figures are beyond our comprehension and cease to have any meaningful impact. First of all, everyone dies, and everyone dies of something, so what difference does it make if it's smoking that kills you or old age, or something else? What is more compelling is how much less life you can expect to live when you smoke. Obviously, the data on this can only generalize, but as a smoker, even with the kindest of assessments you can expect to lose quite a few years off your life span. But we don't really need to go into the figures, it's just plain common sense. Your body is your vehicle through life. The harder you drive it, the less careful you are of it, the more you smash it around, the quicker it's going to conk out. Putting a poison into yourself numerous times a day every day isn't going to increase your life span. You may be strong, weak, fit, unfit, or whatever, but smoking and vaping aren't going to help you live longer. What is perhaps far more horrific to have to face up to than the substantially decreased longevity, is the detriment to the quality of our lives as highlighted in the following statistic: for every person who dies because of smoking, at least thirty people live with a serious smoking-related illness.

People who die of smoking don't just keel over in their late middle age and die; they start wearing out way before that. Health issues like chronic bronchitis and emphysema are crippling; both of these essentially result in your lungs not working properly so you can't get the oxygen you need. People who suffer from these diseases are literally drowning; their lungs cannot provide the oxygen that their body needs. Any kind of physical activity becomes increasingly difficult and many of them are confined to bed or wheelchairs. The average life expectancy of someone diagnosed with emphysema is five years, which means that if you get it you can expect to live with its crippling effects for around five years before you become one of that year's 480,000 people who die from smoking.

The point is that smoking not only shortens your life, it also ruins it. And it ruins it for years before it finally kills you. Smoking isn't about just accepting a shorter life, it's about accepting a ruined life. So when does it start impacting your lifestyle? The answer is right now, even before now, right when you had that very first cigarette. Because even back then it increased your heart rate and made you feel physically heavier and lacking in energy. And that negative impact just increases and increases until it finally kills you. Given all of this, one question that is just begging to be asked is "Why is it still legal?"

One of the reasons for this is its prevalence. To make a law you have to have the power to enforce it. If a lot of people have an interest in breaking it, then you've got to be able to allocate significant resources to enforcing it. Look at the lesson of Prohibition; making something that was popular illegal just encouraged widespread breaches of the law and gave more money to the organized crime syndicates that profited from supplying alcohol. It encouraged widespread disrespect for the law.

Another important reason is, as ever, money. The estimates for the legal global tobacco market in 2018 indicate that sales were worth approximately $814 billion. The global vaping market was valued at about $14.05 billion in 2018 and was expected to grow to $29.39 billion through 2022. That's doubling in four years. That's an awful lot of profit for some very wealthy organizations, and an awful lot of tax being funneled to the government, to say nothing of the money that goes to support the economy generally.

Fortunately, though, this is one of the areas where the might of these corporate and governmental behemoths can have zero power over you. After all, all their clever political and financial positioning, all their ingenious moves and resourceful tactics and legal wrangling can have absolutely no impact on you if you no longer purchase their products. If you do that, their effect on you is zilch. Consider this: if everyone were to stop purchasing their products, those corporate entities would either die or (more likely) morph into something entirely different (some large tobacco players diversified into a range of non-tobacco goods and services in the 1960s to 1990s). After all, if you can sell something that ruins lives and kills people and has absolutely zero benefits, how good must you be at selling something that is actually useful?

The fact is that corporate might cannot force you to smoke or vape, and if you quit you very quickly start to gain what you have lost. As soon as you finish that last cigarette, the very second you stop the supply of nicotine, something wonderful starts to happen: the healing process begins. As the nicotine leaves your system your heart rate and blood pressure drop. Some people will tell you that your heart rate will "return to normal" after about twenty minutes; and it *will* drop, but it won't go back to how it would be had you never smoked because smoking actually erodes your fitness, and to get your fitness back takes time.

We've mentioned briefly before how nicotine increases the heart rate, let's now take a minute to examine how this impacts our fitness.

The word *fitness* is one of those words that people often use without any proper understanding of what it means. Most people understand that it means that you are better able to take or endure more physical activity at a higher level if you are fit, but have you stopped to think what the actual physical differences are between someone who is fit and someone who is unfit? Fit people tend to have more muscle, but this isn't always the case. Think about a body builder compared to a marathon runner. Who would have the least muscle? Which of them would you bet on to run twenty-six miles in the shortest time?

Interestingly, one of the biggest physical differences between someone who is fit and someone who is unfit is their blood composition. To put it very simply, when your muscles are working hard they need oxygen and nutrients to keep them going. The harder and quicker they're working, the more they need. This oxygen comes into the body through the mouth or nose, into the lungs, where it is then absorbed into the bloodstream and then pumped around the body by the heart.

When your heart rate is regularly being increased by physical activity, two important changes start to take place. First, the red blood cells in your blood, which are the cells that carry the oxygen and nutrients to the muscles, start to die off sooner. At first glance this may not seem like a good thing, but in fact it is. Younger red blood cells can carry more oxygen than older ones, so as the average age of the red blood cells decreases, they are able to carry more oxygen, so your heart has to work less hard, or pump less, to get the required oxygen to your muscles.

The other change is that the concentration of red blood cells increases, so there are more of them in your blood.

The practical upshot of this is that as you get fitter there are more blood cells carrying more oxygen getting to your muscles with each pump of the heart. Imagine that a muscle needs one unit of oxygen per second to run. Each pump of the heart delivers half a unit, so your heart has to pump twice a second to get the oxygen there. But if the blood cells have a younger average age (so that they carry more oxygen), and if each pump of the heart gets more cells to the muscle (because the concentration of cells is greater), that muscle may get that unit of oxygen in just one pump. So, instead of having to pump 120 times a minute, your heart only has to pump 60 times a minute.

This is what happens if you are regularly increasing your heart rate through physical activity. But what if you're regularly increasing it without the associated physical activity? What if you use a drug to keep increasing your heart rate? Well, in that case, the opposite happens.

Say you are sitting totally still, and your heart is getting all the oxygen that your muscles need to them by pumping 60 times a minute. You then take a drug that doubles your heart rate. Your blood is then transporting twice as much oxygen as is needed; there's a massive surplus. So the opposite happens to when you get fit; in this case, stimulation with a drug means you get unfit. The concentration of red blood cells in the blood decreases, and your red blood cells aren't replaced with new blood cells so quickly (so that the average age of them increases and they can carry less oxygen).

This is the knock-off effect of smoking on fitness and energy levels, and it is huge. If you smoke and want to exercise you are already at a huge disadvantage. Because of your elevated heart rate you've already got far less fuel in the tank in terms of potential heart rate increase than if you had never smoked, and over the days, weeks, months, and years your fitness is being further and further eroded and destroyed. This is why, along with cancer and respiratory disease, heart disease is one of the big killers for smokers. When you smoke or vape, every movement puts more pressure on your heart as it has to beat faster to get your oxygen-depleted blood around your body.

But when you finally quit, every time you accelerate your heart rate through exercise you become stronger and fitter, and with no chemical acceleration of the heart rate, the rapid erosion of your fitness ceases. And when I say exercise, I don't mean that you have to go for a twenty-mile run, just walking around the house doing your usual daily activities is enough. The human body is a phenomenally robust and adaptable machine (and moreover is one that self-heals if it just has the right fuel) and although it will take time and will vary from individual to individual, with a bit of gentle exercise many people can get their resting heart rate to roughly where it ought to be within a couple of months or even a few weeks after quitting smoking.

So what else happens when you stop smoking? The nicotine will leave your system and is entirely gone in three days, but the chemical imbalance that it leaves behind takes a bit longer to be rectified. The physical withdrawal usually peaks at around the five-day mark and tails off completely after about three weeks.

Research has revealed that when you quit nicotine, you can expect to experience many milestones for health improvements over time, things like:

- After one day, your blood pressure drops and your circulation improves, cutting your risk of heart disease.
- After a month, the healing of your lungs significantly reduces shortness of breath and coughing.
- After nine months, cilia (small hairs inside your lungs that act like a filtering system to protect your lungs, which become damaged by smoking) recover from the effects of cigarette smoke.
- After a year, your risk of coronary heart disease is cut in half, and will continue to decrease.
- After ten years, you've cut your chances of dying from lung cancer in half, and dramatically reduced your likelihood of getting mouth, throat, or pancreatic cancer.
- After twenty years, your risk of dying from a smoking-related cause is now as low as someone who has never smoked a cigarette in their life.

These important facts are all great, but for me quitting wasn't about these milestones, it was about two very simple, undeniable truths:

First, that smoking was ruining my quality of life here and now. That was key for me. When I saw through the illusion that smoking was pleasurable and improved my life, when I realized that every single inhalation made me feel worse than had I never smoked, that even the great "pleasure" of that first cigarette of the day was nothing to how I would feel all the time after I quit, and when I realized that how I felt all the time—heavy, slow, and lethargic—wasn't normal and was caused by my smoking, and that quitting would leave me feeling energetic, bright, and positive, it was a major turning point.

Second, I understood that the moment I quit smoking my body and brain would start to heal. Within a few weeks I would feel better than I had in all the years I had been smoking. It might take one, two, five, ten, or twenty years to fully heal. I might never make it, but the key was that I would be far, far better off for stopping. In fact, it wasn't even the case that I would have to wait for the withdrawal to pass before I felt better. When you understand the nature of cravings you are better off the second you finish your last ever dose of nicotine.

We will deal with cravings in detail later on, but for now let's stick to the physiological side. Sure, you might feel a bit woolly-headed, a bit out of sorts, a bit like something is missing (which it is) or that there is something you need to be doing but aren't doing, but on the other hand you've finally solved your biggest problem, and things will now get better and better. Of course you'll have bad days, everybody does, but you'll be stronger, physically and mentally, and better able to deal with them. Those dark clouds that have been hanging over you, that cognitive dissonance, will lighten until they are truly gone, always and forever.

9.

Is Breathing In Smoke Enjoyable?

A lot of people struggle with the concept that there is nothing inherently enjoyable about breathing in smoke or vapor. For smokers and vapers, it's seen as almost the third way of consuming something for pleasure. You eat food, you drink drinks, and you inhale smoke or vapor. Let's now bring this out of our subconscious and shine the light of reason on it. To do this right, it's helpful to run through a quick overview of the human respiratory system.

Obviously human beings need oxygen to survive. It is our lungs that extract oxygen from the air and send it into our bloodstream. What we need to consider is how that air gets inside our bodies and into our lungs in the first place.

There are two ways for air to get into our lungs. The first is via our nose. The nose isn't just a passageway through which airs travels, it's actually a lot more. It has extremely sensitive sensors to detect exactly what we are breathing in (this is, in essence, our sense of smell). It provides us with very important information about the world around us. It can warn us about fire, if food has gone bad, or if something is good to eat. So on the one hand it provides us with information about the world around us. But it has another function, and that is to make sure that the air we are breathing in is not poisonous.

If the air that we are breathing is poisonous, this will trigger an extreme motor reaction. Our nose may sting, our eyes water, and we will involuntarily shy away from it in an attempt to find a cleaner, purer air source.

The human nose isn't just equipped with sensors, it is also equipped with defense mechanisms designed to remove any impurities that may be in the air. It has fine hairs on the inside of it and it also generates mucus. The combination of these two defenses traps any tiny particles that may be in the air so as to prevent them from entering your lungs.

This is all well and good, but this defense mechanism is where one of the problems with the nose as a source of air comes in. The tubes have to be fairly narrow so that any particles are effectively trapped; if the tubes were too wide, a significant number of particles would just pass through them. The sinuses are also susceptible to infection (which is what the common cold is). When an infection takes hold, the sinuses swell up as more blood is directed to that area so that the white blood cells in the blood can fight the infection. This causes our nose to become blocked. The nose also sticks out a bit and is therefore susceptible to injury, and injury can cause it to swell up and therefore get blocked, as anyone who has had a broken nose, or even a sharp crack on it, can testify. There are also times, of course, during intense physical activity that the amount of oxygen we need to keep up with the activity in question exceeds the amount that can fit down the narrow passages of the nose. For all these reasons we have a secondary way of getting air into our lungs—through our mouths.

Breathing through your mouth allows a far greater amount of air to make it into your lungs. The passageway to the lungs in your throat is wider, unconstrained by hairs, and provides a shorter, more direct route to the lungs. It is also less susceptible to injury and far less likely to close up through infection. So it allows more air to get down into your lungs far quicker. The downside? It has a far more basic sensor and defense mechanism than the nose has (which is why people hold their nose when they smell something unpleasant; by breathing through their mouth they bypass their sense of smell and can't detect the foul smell). If there is a bad smell in the air you will notice it if you breathe through your nose, but you are less likely to if you breathe through your mouth. To breathe something in through your mouth and still trigger a reaction, it has to be extremely unpleasant and even poisonous to trigger a coughing reaction, like taking a whole lungful of bonfire smoke.

This may seem like an odd system, but in fact it works extremely well. Most of the time breathing through the nose is perfectly adequate—we get the oxygen we need and it is properly filtered. On the odd occasion when the route through the nose isn't adequate—either we need more oxygen than will fit through the narrower passageways of the nose, or we have a cold and our nose is blocked—we have the mouth as backup.

This alternative route through the mouth may not be able to filter out all the impurities, but that's fine, the lungs can deal with that small amount of particles and impurities with absolutely no detrimental impact at all since the lungs themselves have their own limited defense mechanisms that are designed to kick in on those occasions when we need to obtain oxygen by the secondary backup route through the mouth. They might struggle to cope if we did this all the time, but occasional use is absolutely fine.

So now we have a basic understanding of how our respiratory system works: the nose is the primary method for taking in air, complete with sensor and filtering system. The mouth is the secondary system with a far more basic sensor and filtering system. The lungs have their own limited defense mechanism that is designed to cope with the odd occasion of increased physical activity or illness or injury, when inhalation through the nose becomes difficult.

So how does all this help us understand whether breathing in smoke or vapor is inherently enjoyable? Just consider the facts. First off, people don't smoke or vape through their nose. Smokers do occasionally get some smoke directly up their nose, and it's the nasal equivalent of rubbing your eyes when you've been handling chilies. It is deeply unpleasant. Just to be clear here, I am not talking about the smell of tobacco smoke in the air, where it is diluted in clear air several thousand times over; I am talking about it in its undiluted state, the state it is in when it goes into your lungs, when a wisp of smoke makes its way directly into your nose. And if you vape and you think you are safe because it is the various chemicals and compounds in the cigarette smoke that are the problem, I'm afraid it is not as simple as that. Sniffing vapor up your nose is just as unpleasant as sniffing cigarette smoke. In fact, what most people find is that nicotine-free varieties of vapor can be sniffed up the nose, but any vape with nicotine in it causes an unpleasant adverse effect. This is because nicotine itself is a poison. This is something we will come back to later in the book, but for now all you need to bear in mind is that smoking or vaping through the nose is impossible; we humans are only able to physically stand inhaling smoke or vapor because we have this secondary method of getting air into our lungs, which has far fewer sensors than our nose.

So as far as inhaling nicotine-laden vapor or smoke goes, it isn't enjoyable; in fact, it's only possible because we have a secondary inhalation system that allows us to bypass the sensors in our nose that tell us when something we are inhaling is poison.

However, despite this fact, many people find they cough and splutter when they take their first ever breath of smoke or vapor (if it contains nicotine). Why is this? It is because that even when we are bypassing the vast majority of the sensors, nicotine is still a highly poisonous chemical and the usual reaction is for the lungs to trigger a coughing reaction.

So most people's bodies react to that very first inhalation by rejecting it; we cough and splutter as our lungs try to reject the smoke or vapor. But what happens directly after that is key. Even when we cough and splutter, some of that nicotine makes it into our lungs, where it goes into our bloodstream, and immediately we feel more alert and more focused due to the stimulating effect of the nicotine. Your subconscious doesn't realize that what has happened isn't actually good for you, it doesn't realize that the drug may make you feel better but is in fact poisoning you; all it works on is cause and effect. All it learns from the experience is that something it originally thought was unpleasant and to be avoided (in this case inhaling smoke) actually seemed to confer a beneficial effect (we feel more alert and focused). And so starts a new learning process: the process of addiction. With every subsequent inhalation of nicotine our subconscious is learning, and having re-emphasized, a very important lesson: inhaling this poison is actually "good."

Over the next few days, weeks, and months, as long as we keep inhaling nicotine, our brain starts to learn the lesson that as one dose wears off, we feel anxious and out of sorts and unpleasant. When we start to feel this feeling, our brain instinctively triggers the desire for another dose. So whenever you start to feel anxious or out of sorts, whether that feeling comes from the withdrawal or from the usual stresses that life throws up generally, your brain will trigger the desire to inhale some smoke to alleviate that feeling.

This is the pleasure in inhaling nicotine. It only appears pleasurable because it is how we relieve the nicotine withdrawal. Think about the dipper, when every pinch of dip makes their gum burn and sting, but that burning, stinging feeling is a sweet and pleasurable feeling because the brain has reinterpreted in it light of the immediate physical response— which is to relieve the pain of withdrawal.

ENGAGEMENT POINT

There are nicotine-free cigarettes out there, and nicotine-free e-liquids. Many people find they just don't enjoy them the same way they enjoy the nicotine varieties. Have you tried them? How did it feel to you? Was it enjoyable inhaling smoke or vapor without nicotine in it? Or did it seem unsatisfying and pointless? Nicotine-free vapor can confuse your senses because it does have an actual flavor, which can be pleasant in its own right, but if you do enjoy using a nicotine-free e-liquid, is it the inhaling of the vapor that you are actually enjoying? Or just the taste?

10.

We're Trapped: Cravings

So far we've taken a fairly chemical and physiological analysis of smoking and vaping. We've looked at how nicotine affects us and how we can very easily misinterpret its effects and think that it actually gives us some sort of benefit, when what it is really doing is taking something from us and then partially giving it back to us. Remember how glad you were to have me around when I was giving you $100 every day, but how irritated you were when you realized that for every $100 I was giving you, I was first stealing $200 directly out of your savings account?

However, there's a lot more to smoking and vaping than just this. The human brain is a phenomenally intricate and amazing thing, and there are a few psychological processes that we need to fully understand in order to properly dissect and understand our smoking and vaping behavior. One of the most important of these is called craving.

Anyone who has tried and failed to quit smoking or vaping or dipping (which is virtually anyone who has done it for more than a few months) will be familiar with the concept of craving. It is essentially when we desperately want something and just can't get the thought of it out of our minds. It is about obsessing over something.

Craving is a hugely misunderstood concept. People think of it as something that just happens to them and over which they have no control. It's like being hit by a meteorite (only far more likely) in that it is something that just plummets out of the sky and hits us and there is nothing we can do to avoid it. But of course this isn't the case at all, craving is an entirely internal mental process and, moreover, one that happens entirely in our conscious, as opposed to our subconscious, mind. Let's now examine the craving process and then see how it feeds into our smoking and vaping behavior.

Human thoughts aren't static; they tend to follow a path. You may be sitting at your kitchen table, alone, having your morning cup of coffee, just letting you thoughts wander. You may start off thinking about what you have to do that morning, which may lead you to thinking about lunch and maybe meeting a friend. Your friend may be going through a rough patch, so you may then start thinking about what he or she is experiencing, and so on.

For the smoker or vaper, particularly for the smoker or vaper who is making an attempt to quit, it is almost certain that the thought of a smoke will enter his or her head at some point. Take the example of drinking a cup of coffee each morning. For the last five, ten, or even twenty years, if you are a smoker or vaper, you may have been drinking coffee every day with a smoke, so thinking of smoking at that time is natural. The thought is stronger if you are in the first few days of quitting, when the discomfort of withdrawal is at its most significant, because at this point both your conscious and subconscious will be screaming at you to have a smoke, and you feel awful, disoriented, unfocused, out of sorts, and dozy. It's telling you that smoking will make you feel focused, confident, content, and satisfied.

So, the thought of having a smoke or a vape inevitably enters a person's mind. This in and of itself does not create a craving; there are in fact five separate stages in the thought process that happen starting with the "thought moment"—the first stage—when the craving starts to kick in and really starts to bite.

The next stage, after the thought of smoking has entered our mind, is fantasizing. This is when our imagination kicks in. The thought of smoking or vaping has entered our mind, and so we start to fantasize about how it would feel to smoke or vape. We test it out in our mind. We sit back and imagine how it would feel to breath that nicotine into our lungs, about how we would immediately feel more focused, more confident, more able to cope with the day ahead. In essence, we start to torture ourselves. Like the dieter who sits there salivating over the thought of a pizza, we imagine how very pleasurable it would be to take that lungful of smoke or vapor. Forget tobacco advertising, who needs it? Smokers do all the advertising for the tobacco industry themselves. Imagine turning on the TV in this day and age and seeing a commercial showing someone smoking, taking a huge lungful of smoke, and seeing the look of bliss and contentment coming over their face. There'd be uproar. Yet this is what each individual smoker is broadcasting to themselves every single day the world over when they start to crave a smoke.

This is the second part of the craving process, and it is very powerful. Advertisers want to get personal; they want their ads to make every person feel like the ad is about them personally. One of the reasons this part of the process is so powerful is because it is our own personal advertisement. It's like turning on the TV right now and seeing a commercial showing you, at this moment, having a cigarette, and being able to feel how good it feels to smoke it (albeit that the "pleasure" comes purely from relieving the withdrawal caused by the previous doses). Imagine the outcry if the tobacco and vaping industries developed a way of mapping an individual's thoughts so that they could project, to that individual, right into their mind, an image of them smoking or vaping, showing them looking relaxed and happy and content. Yet, this is exactly what we do to ourselves. This craving step is powerful enough on its own, but it's made even more potent because it's a form of self-imposed torture. We torture ourselves in our imagination.

If you are really busy one day, either at work or at home, you may find you skip lunch; sometimes I even end up skipping breakfast and lunch. Because I'm busy, because I have my mind on other things, because I'm not thinking about eating, I can skip those meals fairly easily. But imagine if you weren't busy, if all you had to do all day was think about food. Imagine if you were sitting in your favorite restaurant all day, with all your favorite dishes laid out in front of you, and all you could do was look at them and smell them and think about how good it would be to tuck into them. That would be unbearable. That would be torture.

This fantasizing is hugely powerful in and of itself, but the next stage, the third in the craving process, can make it even more difficult, and that is entertaining the possibility of having a smoke. This is when we move from fantasizing about smoking on a purely intellectual level, in other words just tentatively imagining what it would be like to smoke, to actually thinking about having one. It is where we consider abandoning our attempt to quit and actually having a smoke.

This makes the torture even more concentrated. It would be torturous enough to sit there in your favorite restaurant, with all your favorite dishes laid out in front of you, but what would be even more unbearable would be to pick up a large slice or spoonful or forkful of something, to raise it to your mouth, to open your mouth, to have the smell of it fill your nostrils . . .

Actually entertaining the possibility of taking that smoke takes the agony of desire to whole new level, because now it is actually within our reach.

There is then a further stage to the process, which has to do with how decision-making takes place in the human mind. There is a substantial amount of evidence that shows that many of our decisions are made in the subconscious mind. What can sometimes happen while the above thought processes are going on, is that your subconscious just decides that you are going to smoke—this is the fourth stage.

Think about some of the subconscious actions we talked about earlier in the book. Think about walking into a dark room when there is a power outage and automatically reaching out to flip the light switch. Isn't it the case that this is far more likely to happen when you've got a million things on your mind? The kids are acting up, work is getting out of hand, you've got an assignment to hand in, your partner is being particularly irritating at the moment, your best friend is being weird, oh, and why the hell did I just flip the light switch when we don't have any power?

The fact of the matter is that the conscious mind deals with what it can, and the subconscious mind picks up the rest. The human brain can only consciously consider a certain number of things at any one time, and when it's overloaded the subconscious is far more likely to step in and start picking up the slack.

As you can see, stages two and three of the craving process—the fantasizing and the entertaining the possibility of having a smoke—take up a huge amount of conscious thought, so it is entirely possible that your subconscious just jumps in to decide (on the basis of a woefully incomplete analysis of the situation, that it feels good so let's do it) that you're going to go right ahead and just smoke. This subconscious decision-making, as noted above, is stage four of the craving process.

When this happens, you will then enter the fifth and final stage of the craving process, what I call "the search for excuses." At this point you've given in, you're going to smoke, that decision has been made by your subconscious and is done with. All that needs to happen now is for your conscious mind to catch up. When this happens, your thought process changes subtly from weighing the pros and cons to a quick sift of the data to find any old excuse to justify the decision to smoke. Because you are literally on the verge of lighting up, the torture is at its most concentrated. You are not making a decision, you are seeking a justification. You will recognize this thought process when it happens because it is panicky, irrational, and in your heart of hearts you know full well you are going to smoke.

Remember, the conscious mind can only consider a certain number of things at one time. I have read a few times that that number is seven, but I expect it probably varies from individual to individual and how deeply they are thinking about any particular thing, but the fact of the matter is that you can only think about a finite number of things at any one time. You may, at this stage, have ten reasons to smoke and ten thousand not to, but because you are just sifting through all of them and holding on to any reason to smoke and discarding any reason not to, at some stage you'll have seven (or however many) reasons to smoke. Because you've got no room left in your mind to consider any reasons *not* to smoke, you've got a load of reasons to smoke and no reasons not to. Job done. You've now justified your decision. You light that cigarette as quickly as you can before the whole process is spoiled by then remembering all the many valid reasons not to smoke.

Imagine you're on trial for murder. You were walking along the street one day and you came across the body of someone who has been murdered, and you end up as the main suspect. You didn't do it, but there's some circumstantial evidence that suggests you might have. You speak to your lawyer and there's a bit of bad news, but a lot of good news. The bad news is that there are seven bits of fairly flimsy evidence that suggest you might have committed the murder. But the good news is that there are more than a hundred bits of evidence to pretty much prove conclusively that you couldn't have committed the murder. So all in all, things are looking pretty good.

However, a few days before the trial you get a visit from your lawyer.

There's more bad news. The entire criminal justice system has been over-hauled. The new system is that the jury is only allowed to be presented with seven pieces of evidence, no more. And all seven pieces are decided by the prosecution.

How do you feel about that? Do you think that's a sensible way to run a justice system? Is that a good and fair way to make a decision? What if you are in a jurisdiction that has the death penalty, and that decision is going to dictate whether you live or you die? Do you think you might be inclined to put a bit of effort into changing that system, so that your life wasn't ruined or ended on the basis of a completely ridiculous and one-sided decision-making process?

Addiction is a prison, and being forced to keep taking a poison that is killing you is a death sentence.

Here again are the five possible stages to craving:

1. The thought
2. Fantasizing
3. Considering the possibility of smoking
4. Subconscious decision-making
5. The search for excuses

You may not go through all of these. You may just fantasize about having a smoke, then have one, or decide you're not going to waste time thinking about it; or you may get distracted by work or kids or friends and be able to abandon the entire craving process. Alternatively, you may fantasize, entertain the possibility of smoking, then smoke, or get distracted, or remind yourself forcefully of all the reason you quit in the first place and again manage to abandon the whole process. But it is worth being aware of the entire process because it not only shows what you are up against, but also demonstrates that it isn't something that just hits us and that we are powerless against; it is a conscious thought process and, moreover, one that presents numerous opportunities to disrupt and defeat it.

Now that we've dissected this process and we've got it laid out in front of us, there are a few points worth making about it, the first of which is that it isn't pleasant.

Whether you are fantasizing about having something that you are denying yourself, agonizing over whether to give in and smoke, or frantically searching for excuses to do something you know you are far better off not doing, it isn't a pleasant process. Not only is it decidedly unpleasant in and of itself, but it stops you concentrating on anything else you might be doing. Think back to the beginning of this chapter when we gave the example of sitting and having your morning cup of coffee. That would ordinarily be a pleasant experience, but if you start craving a smoke you will no longer be enjoying your morning cup of coffee. You will no longer be appreciating the peace and quiet and the taste of the coffee, because your attention is entirely taken up with an unpleasant internal process—an argument with yourself.

The same is true of any situation. You may be at work trying to concentrate, with friends trying to relax, with your kids trying to enjoy some family time, with your partner, sitting down at the end of a hard day, having a nice meal. Whatever it might be, you are no longer enjoying the situation you're in; in fact, you may as well be sitting in a prison cell for all the attention you're paying to what is going on around you, because all your attention is focused inward, thinking about how sweet it would be to smoke.

So it's an unpleasant and distracting process, and the quickest and easiest way of ending it is to just smoke the wretched thing and be done with it. Win, lose, or draw—and we know it's always lose—once that cigarette is lit and you're smoking away, the entire craving process ends; after all, you don't fantasize about something and agonize over whether to have it when you're in the process of consuming it. As soon as it's lit, the craving process ends and you can get back to enjoying that cup of coffee, that time with your friends, kids, that meal, and so forth. At this stage the cigarette is a placebo, but a very powerful one, and it can mean the difference between engaging with and enjoying life, and just suffering it. This is one of the reasons that smoking, vaping, and dipping can end up having such a huge hold over us, but in fact, for this aspect at least, it is purely psychological.

When we understand this craving process in a bit more detail we can also understand how it is possible for smokers and vapers (even those at the higher end of the physical addiction scale) to sometimes abstain for extended periods or even quit totally with relative ease.

A dipper or a smoker may go to the cinema or theater, they may go out for a meal, they may go on a flight or visit a friend or relative where they can't smoke. Some may go to the hospital for a few nights, or have a bad cold or flu and stop for a few days with little or no aggravation. They may become pregnant and stop immediately. The reason that nicotine addicts are able to do this without going to pieces is that their circumstances may prevent them from going into a craving cycle.

If you are unlucky enough to end up in the hospital for a few nights, and for whatever reason are confined to your bed, smoking or vaping is simply not an option. Because there is absolutely no possibility of our being able to do it, we are less likely to start fantasizing about it, and even if we do fantasize about it, we never entertain the possibility of actually having a smoke *because we know it isn't possible. It simply isn't an option.*

So you may lay there and think that it would be nice to have a smoke, you may very much look forward to having one as soon as you are discharged, but you never refine and concentrate the torture by entertaining the possibility of having one because having one is simply not possible. Smoking is off the menu. Your subconscious is also not going to unilaterally make the decision to smoke, because that option isn't on the table. It is the certainty of the situation that is key here, it makes stages three, four, and five of the craving process impossible, and it often very much decreases the chance of stage two initializing. After all, a lot of people won't even fantasize about smoking if it simply isn't possible.

There is another psychological process that comes into play when we smoke that we need to be aware of, that of cognitive dissonance—a process in which you want two completely contradictory things at the same time.

When people smoke or vape they often feel trapped by something that they can't stop. Health aspects aside, most people recognize that they need this thing to cope with and enjoy life, that life just doesn't seem so sweet or enjoyable without it. But they also know that their lives were complete and that they enjoyed themselves perfectly well before they started smoking or vaping. They may make all sort of excuses about the health aspect being overstated, or that they stand a better than average chance of being immune to the health effects, or that the enjoyments out-weighs the risks, or that "everything seems to be bad for you these days," but most people know deep down that these are just excuses and that they're in the grip of something unpleasant. So a part of them desperately wants to stop, but another part of them desperately wants to carry on, to not be deprived of this little grain of comfort in an otherwise cruel and unforgiving world.

This is what cognitive dissonance is: wanting two entirely different and contradictory things, in this case to both continue smoking, and to stop doing it.

The natural reaction to cognitive dissonance is to just try to ignore it, to just bury anything that reminds us of it. The trouble is that we can never bury it entirely. Every time we cough or have a sore throat, every time we realize how much money we're spending, every time we can't smoke and just sit there obsessing about it instead of enjoying the moment, that cognitive dissonance becomes apparent. Even when we are able to ignore it, it is still there, at the back of our mind, or like a weight on our back, constantly dragging us down. It's exhausting and debilitating, and we waste valuable time and effort thinking and worrying about it. It's like picking up a heavy weight and carrying it around with you your whole life. You may get used to it, and on the odd occasion forget it's there, but forgetting it's there doesn't mean it isn't there. It will always be there, weighing you down, like Jacob Marley's ghost draped in chains in Charles Dickens's *A Christmas Carol*, making every step more difficult. Until you finally come to the point that you can let it go, and finally be free.

11.

Smoking Relieves Stress

The idea that smoking or vaping relieves stress is such a basic one that a lot of people just take it for granted, and it would never even dawn on them to question it. It's not even something you can argue against, is it? We all know from thousands of personal experiences that we feel less stressed when we smoke. But does this necessarily mean that smoking actually alleviates stress? Think again about me giving you $100 every day then finding out that for every $100 I gave you, I'd already stolen $200 from your savings account. Was I actually giving you anything? Did you end up wealthier overall, or worse off?

This is another area where it can be useful to illustrate the points with reference to some simple graphs. Remember that as soon as you put out a cigarette or stop vaping, the nicotine starts to leave your body and the withdrawal starts to build up. It's a subtle feeling but not a pleasant one. Think about that causeway, getting narrower and narrower. As the nicotine wears off we start to feel less confident and not quite with it. It's a very similar feeling to the ordinary stresses and strains of everyday life, to such an extent that it's very hard to differentiate between the two.

So let's now assume that you are a smoker or a vaper and you've had an argument with your partner or friend, or you've got an assignment to hand in, or you have a problem at work or college or school, or you car's broken down or you're short of money, or any one of the other million things that happen to every human being every day and that form part of the ups and downs of life. Whatever it is, imagine that it causes you stress. The graph below shows your stress level from 1 to 10. The black is the genuine stress causes by the event in question; the light gray is the additional stress that you are suffering because of your nicotine addiction.

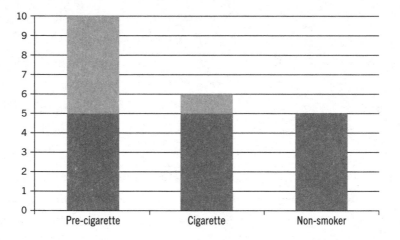

As you can see, the first column is the moment before we take that dose of nicotine. We are suffering 10 points of stress, 5 from the event and 5 from the fact that we are addicted to nicotine. We cannot differentiate between the two; all we know is we are stressed and we assign all the stress to the event in question.

The second column is when we smoke a cigarette. As you can see, the overall stress is substantially reduced; this is because in taking another dose of nicotine, we are relieving the stress that is directly caused by the physical withdrawal. Again, we cannot differentiate between the stress due to the event and the stress due to the withdrawal. All we know is that the stress has been substantially reduced. The cigarette therefore seems to have eased the situation dramatically. But in fact, all it has done is exaggerated the problem by adding additional stress, and then has partially relieved that additional stress.

What is noticeable here is that there is still an element of additional stress even while we are smoking that cigarette. As we've covered previously, smoking doesn't alleviate all the problems it causes. Even when we are smoking we will suffer the cognitive dissonance and the elevated heart rate (which makes us feel heavy and lethargic). Obviously the effect of these factors on our stress levels will differ from person to person and will also differ as time goes by. The effect smoking has on our heart rate and fitness generally gets progressively worse over time. If you are in your sixties, and have had forty years of regular daily smoking, you are going to be weak and frail compared to if you had never smoked. This feeling of heaviness, of weakness, of lack of fitness, is going to be with you all the time, whether you are smoking or not (and in fact is likely to be marginally worse when you are smoking due to the increased heart rate). The difference in stress points between you as a smoker and you as a non-smoker isn't going to just be 1 or 2 stress points, but many.

This dynamic has far greater implications than just ingraining in us the false belief that smoking or vaping is a good way to relieve stress. Have you ever heard the term "the human condition"? It refers to the characteristics and key life events that are the essentials of human existence and, frankly, its outlook can be a bit dark. Benjamin Franklin once said that "nothing is certain except death and taxes" but Google and Starbucks have proved that in fact only death is certain. No one has any certain knowledge about what happens when we die. Many people have faith in a particular religion, but faith is exactly that, a belief rather than actual knowledge. So the one event we know is going to happen to us is an unknown. What we know about the universe isn't particularly comforting—it's very large and very cold and very dark, and there are large lumps of rock flying around it (the earth's dominant life-form, the dinosaurs, were wiped out when a massive meteor crashed into Mexico's Yucatán Peninsula around 65 million years ago).

Closer to home, we are living on a planet whose natural resources are rapidly running out and, depending on which expert you are listening to on any particular day, is being irreparably damaged by the human life-style. Although we humans like to believe in some kind of universal justice, in reality random death and suffering seem to hit people the world over every day with no rhyme or reason. The most common stages of life for people everywhere are birth, childhood, adolescence, marriage, children, the death of one's parents, and our own deaths. In other words, life starts out OK and gets progressively less pleasant. All of us start off with grand hopes and dreams, but very few of us actually realize those dreams, and even those who do often don't seem to obtain much pleasure or personal satisfaction from it. Thrown in for good measure for many of us are things like divorce, war, accidents, and diseases that spring up seemingly at random to cause death and financial ruin.

However, most of us deal with these central facets of human existence fairly well. Some of us turn to religion, others resign ourselves to it and just try to do what little good we can before our time is up; some meditate or escape into books and films and music. Some of us use a mix of these, and more.

The trouble is that when you're smoking, the same stress dynamic applies. All of us end up at some point going through a depressing and ultimately fruitless contemplation of one or more of these central unpleasant facts that provide the backdrop of human existence. Mostly what we end up doing is shrugging our shoulders because it's nothing we can change, and so we get on with enjoying what we can. We see friends and we laugh and joke with them, we spend time with our friends and loved ones, we keep striving for something better and wringing every ounce of enjoyment from our lives. After all, that's all you can do.

Let's look at the stress graph again, but this time imagine you're going through a contemplative stage, you're thinking about how old your parents are, or how old you are, or how horribly long ago your childhood seems, or how fast your children are growing up, or the damage that's being done to the planet—or any one of the other central truths of human existence. Remember how we spoke earlier about how problems come with a severity rating of 1 to 10, with 1 being the easiest to deal with and 10 being the hardest to cope with? Let's say for the sake of argument that ordinarily you're able to deal happily with anything up to a 6 or 7. With this in mind, look again at the graph below:

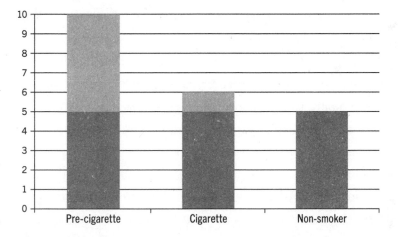

Remember that the black is the genuine stress and the light gray is the additional stress caused by the nicotine.

Can you see how absolutely massively important the cigarette becomes? There you are, thinking about how one day you will die, how you will actually, physically cease to exist, how your mortal remains will either decompose or be burnt, and how the world will just go on as usual—the same stupid advertisements on TV, the same mindless sitcoms, the same petty problems in the office—but all without your existence. It all seems a bit overwhelming. But then you have a cigarette and you are able to shrug it off, to deal with it, to accept it. In this way the cigarette becomes more than just stress relief; in our eyes it becomes our way of being able to cope with and accept the human condition, even to face our own death, to contemplate our parents' deaths, to face the simple fact that time, once passed, can never return.

There is another aspect to this that is even more terrifying. As smoking and vaping erode both our fitness and our ability to cope with the ups and downs of human existence, so life becomes increasingly less pleasant. When smokers reach late middle age, smoking starts to really take its toll. Life just isn't enjoyable anymore, indeed the only pleasure a smoker has is when they smoke a cigarette and relieve, for a few minutes, that horrible feeling of being unable to cope with life. The threat of death, to a smoker, just isn't that terrible because life isn't pleasant for them, so the loss of it holds no real fear. Think about it—the dynamic of deciding to smoke, even though you know it's killing you, isn't just dependent on how desperate you are to continue smoking, but also how awful a thing the loss of your life is. If your life is a constant drag, if it is difficult and exhausting and unpleasant, then death isn't going to look so awful. If, on the other hand, you enjoy life, you love it, you embrace it with energy and enthusiasm, the loss of it is going to be far more awful for you.

The late, great Allen Carr once said that he used to think that smoking removed his fear of death, but that if it did, then it replaced that fear of death with something far more awful: a fear of living.

12.

The Driving Forces: Mental Resilience, Fading Affect Bias, and Ambition

The usual way to go about quitting smoking is to list all the reasons you want to stop, grit your teeth, and wait for the desire to smoke to slowly fade away. It would never dawn on most people to start also looking at the reasons they *do* smoke, because they don't suspect that these reasons are not rooted in reality.

The problem is that there are a few reasons why it is your resolution to quit, rather than your desire to smoke, that fades as time goes by. The reasons behind this phenomenon have to do with mental resilience, Fading Affect Bias, and ambition, and we are going to consider all three of these in this chapter. These roadblocks are all simple things to avoid *if you are aware of them*. Like many things in life, they can trip you up if you're not expecting them, but if you are expecting them, you are prepared.

1. Mental Resilience

We've already covered in some detail how nicotine withdrawal erodes our natural mental resilience and confidence. But one particular aspect of this that we really need to be aware of is how, in that frail state, our natural tendency is to shy away from difficult, problematic things, to put them off to another day when we feel more confident and better able to cope.

Remember, when you are at your best, mentally and physically, you will also be at your most confident and you will feel most capable. That is the time you feel best able to grapple with difficult problems. Have you ever dragged yourself into work when you've had a hangover or when you've been ill and should really have had a day off sick? Did you fly through the day and get through all your work enthusiastically? Or did you end up doing a third of what you'd usually do, and that being only the very easy stuff?

When we don't feel right, we have a natural tendency to want to hide away somewhere safe until we feel better, to put off problems and not to get stuck in them.

When we quit smoking, almost immediately withdrawal starts to kick in and with it comes a feeling of insecurity that makes us want to put off anything difficult. And what's the most difficult thing we're facing at that time? You've guessed it, it's quitting smoking!

If you've tried to quit smoking or vaping before now, then think back to your previous attempt(s). Did you just decide you were going to abandon your attempt to stop and then just continue to smoke all day, every day until you dropped dead in your fifties? Or did you just decide that you would stop, yes, but that it just wasn't the right time?

There is a marked tendency, when people try to quit smoking or vaping, to start off all fired up and confident, but then to start to doubt their decision and in particular to feel that they've picked the wrong time. This isn't just an excuse; there is a physiological reason for this, which is that as the withdrawal kicks in we feel less and less able to deal with difficult things and more and more inclined to put them off until we feel stronger mentally. Our confidence and determination to quit can therefore erode when the withdrawal kicks in.

2. Fading Affect Bias

Fading Affect Bias (FAB) essentially describes the process whereby good memories persist longer than bad ones, or more accurately, the tendency to view events in the past in a more positive light as time passes. It is interesting because it is universal, which means it exists in all human societies, and isn't something that is the product of one culture or another.

What FAB actually means is that our memory of the past tends to become warped and we tend to think of past events as being far more enjoyable and positive then they were when we were experiencing them. We also tend to focus in on the parts that we enjoyed, as opposed to the parts that were less enjoyable. So when you think back on the past, you tend to think about the enjoyable times, as opposed to the times that were humdrum or less fun.

No one really knows why there is this tendency in human beings to view past events in a positive light, but generally it is seen as a good thing. It helps us believe that our lives are more gratifying and pleasant than perhaps they have been, and helps us retain a more positive outlook on life generally.

The trouble is that, again, a natural and largely positive phenomenon in human existence can work against us where drugs are concerned. When we are taking a drug, we're living with the reality of it. The expense, the lack of energy, that unpleasant feeling that we're being forced to do something that we would be far better off without. So we make an attempt to quit. After a few days we start to feel much better, our brain chemistry gets back to normal, leaving us brighter and more confident and positive. Overall, we're massively better off. But at the same time, as our smoking fades into the past, we start to see it slightly differently. Slowly but surely we start to think less and less about the lack of energy, the health worries, the dull, heavy feeling. In short, we stop remembering the reality of smoking. Instead, we start to recall those few occasions where smoking seemed particularly crucial to us, or when we really found it enjoyable.

So Fading Affect Bias is a great thing generally, but it can work against us when we are trying to give something up. The longer we do without something, the more we forget how dreadful it was to be in its grip.

3. Ambition

We usually associate ambition with careers, but here we are going to use it in its wider meaning: the desire of all living creatures (not just human beings) to improve their lives. The desire to improve your life, and the life of your family and species generally, is a basic driving force, like hunger and the desire to reproduce. But it's actually made up of two separate parts: the tendency to be critical of what we have, and to idolize what we don't have.

Have you ever been desperately in love with someone, moved heaven and earth to be with them, then found out that they weren't the perfect human being you thought they were? Have you ever been desperate to get a job, or new place to live, and sat there fantasizing about how your life would be so much better if you could get there, only to find that after a year or two you're already looking for the next move?

This is all to do with how our view of reality isn't reality at all. It's just our perception of reality. People aren't perfect, and neither are jobs and houses. But when we don't have them, and yet we want them, we see only their qualities and not their faults. The complete opposite is true when we possess something, particularly if we've had it for a while. We stop seeing all the positives and start more and more to concentrate on the negatives.

Generally speaking, this is no bad thing; it drives us to keep improving our lives, to always be on the lookout for the next step we can take to make things better. But when it comes to smoking and addiction, it can really work against us.

When we smoke, we are living with the reality of it. It's expensive, we're tired and lethargic all the time, our fitness levels are at rock bottom (even if not in comparison to other people's, certainly to where they would be if we weren't smoking), and even if we believe we genuinely enjoy it, we now worry because there is a drug that we've found ourselves having to take in order to cope with and enjoy life, and we worry about our health. In short, we want out, so we try to quit.

The problem is that as soon as we quit, smoking moves from the "I have it" category into the "I don't have it" category, and instead of seeing the reality of it we start fantasizing about it.

It's useful at this stage to pause for a moment and think in a bit more detail about our smoking and vaping, because all cigarettes aren't created equal. By this I mean that they are not all equally enjoyable. In fact, no cigarette is genuinely enjoyable (the "enjoyment" being the relieving of an unpleasant, disagreeable feeling), but smokers and vapers alike do suffer from the illusion of enjoying them. And no one ever enjoys all of them equally.

Think about your smoking or vaping habits. On any day, which ones do you enjoy most out of all of them? For most people it's the first of the day. Then you may have memories of specific occasions where you really enjoyed one, like sitting on a balcony on holiday, or after a meal, or after finishing a particularly long and unpleasant task where you couldn't smoke. All of these occasions tend to have one thing in common: a long delay after the last dose. This makes perfect sense when we understand the mechanism; after all, if the pleasure of smoking is the relieving of the withdrawal, then the worse the withdrawal, the more pleasurable it is to relieve it.

The point is, though, if you smoke twenty cigarettes a day, you may only really enjoy two or three of them. This is something that is worth getting clear in your mind. Let's for the moment divide your cigarettes or smoking occasions into "enjoyable" (the ones you believe you really enjoy) and those that are "maintenance" cigarettes (the ones that you smoke without really being aware of them, or really enjoying them).

A few years ago this was a very common concept, and people readily related to it. The reason is that years ago there were so many more places you could smoke. You could smoke at work at your desk, on building sites, on planes, trains, and buses, you could smoke in cinemas and theaters, in restaurants and bars. These days you can smoke in fewer and fewer places and this often restricts the number of cigarettes that a person can smoke. Because some people are forced to have some quite extended periods between each dose, they can end up believing that they genuinely enjoy every cigarette they smoke.

If you are in this category, then think back to the last time you could smoke unrestrainedly. Maybe you were with friends drinking in someone's backyard, or in an outside smoking area attached to a bar or restaurant. If you are someone who smokes only a few cigarettes a day, and believes you really enjoy each and every one of them, did you stick to that number on that particular day on that particular occasion? Or did you end up smoking multiple times what you'd normally smoke in a day on that occasion alone? And if so, did you still enjoy every single one of those cigarettes equally, or did you find that you smoked the vast majority of them without even being consciously aware that you were smoking them?

Did you just sit there puffing away on your vape almost nonstop without seeming to get any particular pleasure from it?

The point here is that the vast majority of cigarettes that most people smoke are "maintenance" cigarettes. They aren't particularly enjoyable, we just kind of smoke them because that's what we do. But when we quit smoking, do we think of the vast majority of cigarettes that we smoked that we weren't even particularly enjoying? Or do we think of the very few we smoked that we really enjoyed? Because of this tendency to idolize what we don't have, when we think back on our smoking lives we think of that first cigarette of the day that we believed we really enjoyed, but not the fortieth cigarette we chain-smoked while we were drinking—that we either weren't even aware of or even that we found quite repulsive—even though it's those maintenance cigarettes that form the vast majority of our smoking lives.

You may now be thinking that I've just revealed the solution to your problem—how you can have your cake and eat it, too. How you can get all the pleasure of smoking at a fraction of the risk, and not have to go through the horrors of stopping totally. The answer's staring us in the face, isn't it? We just cut out all the maintenance cigarettes and only smoke the so-called enjoyable ones. We'll get all the pleasure at a fraction of the cost and with a fraction of the health risks.

So now let's move on to the next piece of the jigsaw puzzle and really get to grips with whether cutting down or using substitutes is a viable option.

13.

Cutting Down and Substitutes

In an earlier chapter, we discussed how addiction has a physical side of withdrawal and the pleasure of relieving that withdrawal, but that this alone does not define addiction. Addiction is a learning process; it is not just about the physiological act of withdrawal and relief, but also learning on both a conscious and subconscious level that the act of taking the drug (in this case by smoking, vaping, or dipping) is what leads to that relief. Nicotine withdrawal is unpleasant, but it's a subtle and often hard feeling to pin down. It's very similar to feeling nervous about something, or having a cold and finding it hard to focus. You may experience it when you first smoke, but you may not even realize it's there and it would certainly never occur to your subconscious mind to reach for another smoke to relieve it. Because of this we don't crave a smoke, because the knowledge that the cigarette will relieve the withdrawal hasn't yet been cemented into our subconscious mind. That comes with time and with repeated use. So when we first start smoking, most of us do indeed go through a stage of being able to genuinely take them or leave them. We suffer the withdrawal, but because we are consuming less nicotine it is less severe;

but more importantly, we just live with it. We don't instinctively reach for a cigarette to relieve it. This may mean that we can go for long periods not craving. But this doesn't necessarily mean that we don't crave at all. Let me give you an example.

Say you're a weekday worker and a weekend drinker, and when you drink you also smoke. So you've been through a weekend drinking and smoking. The weekend ends. The withdrawal is there, but it's also mixed up with a lot of other sensations—maybe you're a bit hungover, a bit tired, a bit groggy. So you go to work Monday morning and you don't feel right. A part of it might be an actual hangover but a significant part of it is nicotine withdrawal. But you just see it as your Monday morning feeling, a bit groggy, a bit hungover. That's just Monday mornings, right? It's what everyone has, don't they?

The key is that although the withdrawal is there, it simply wouldn't cross your mind to light up. You only smoke on the weekend, you'd never smoke during the week, you only smoke when you're drinking, so although you may think about smoking (you may see people smoking outside your office as you arrive at work) you would never start fantasizing about having a cigarette, still less would you entertain the possibility of actually having a smoke, *so you don't crave.* You can quite happily go all week without smoking.

So you work your way through the week. As the days move on through Monday, Tuesday, Wednesday, you feel better and better. Your brain chemistry gets back to its normal level, and the withdrawal slowly dissipates. By the time Friday comes around you're in a far better state than you were on Monday, and you have far less (if any) withdrawal to relieve.

So Friday afternoon finally comes, the working day ends, and you head to the bar. You grab a drink and head out to the smoking area. You sit down, take out a cigarette, put it in your mouth, flick your lighter, and raise it to the tip of your cigarette.

Imagine how you'd react if, at that exact moment, someone grabbed the cigarette out of your mouth, snatched the pack, and sprinted off. Apart from the obvious shock, you'd be in a frenzy to try to get another cigarette lit and in your mouth as soon as possible. You'd be just as desperate to get some cigarette smoke into your lungs as a thirty-year daily smoker.

So why can you be fine not smoking all week, then desperate at the weekend? The difference is the craving process, specifically the torture of anticipation. If you know 100 percent that you aren't going to smoke, then there is no anticipation, which is a major part of the craving process.

The problem is that these circumstances that lead us to smoking only in certain situations don't usually last. Sometimes they do, sometimes they may go on for years, but usually something will come along to change things.

Let's go back to our weekend smoker, our weekday worker. This routine may go on for years, decades even, but chances are something will come along at some point to derail it. Maybe one day our worker breaks up with her boyfriend, or has a big argument with her best friend, or finds out that her job's under threat. Maybe she finds out she's going to be thrown out of her house, or she's got a massive expense suddenly that she can't cover. She's worried and upset. It's Wednesday afternoon. Her smoking friend is about to go out for a smoke. She's upset and worried and she just wants something to take the edge off it. So she goes out with her smoking friend and has a cigarette.

A simple act with massive, lifelong consequences. Because a few things happen.

First, the cigarette does help her, because it relieves the withdrawal that is still hanging around from the weekend. So she feels better for having a smoke.

Second, she's just removed the mental barrier against smoking during the week that she had in place for so many years.

Third, from here on in, whenever she feels anxious during the week (which is going to happen lot given she already suffers nicotine withdrawal during the week) she'll remember the time she had a cigarette and that it made her feel better. She will start to think about how it would feel to have another one, how it would make her feel relaxed and confident and able to deal with whatever is bugging her. Then she'll start wondering whether she should actually have one. In other words, she'll be craving a smoke.

This is just an example, and there are a lot of different dynamics here. Our worker may be someone who has a very strong mental barrier against smoking during the week so that she doesn't smoke even when she's having a really bad day, or she may do it once, then stop. But the point is that the natural tendency is to slip into smoking on more and more occasions, and each time we smoke in a different scenario it makes it easier and easier to do it on the next occasion. It's like the valves we have in our veins that allow blood to flow one way and not the other.

This is what smoking, vaping, dipping, or any addiction is. It's a one-way street. We can go forward but we can't go back. Once we learn on a conscious and subconscious level that the unpleasant feeling that builds up after we finish one dose of nicotine can be relieved by another dose, we are through the "take it or leave it" stage and we can never return to it. We can learn that another dose of nicotine will relieve that unpleasant feeling that builds up as soon as the last dose ends, but we can never unlearn it. We may stop for a week, a month, a year, ten years, or fifty years, but ever after, as soon as we light a cigarette, finish it, and the nicotine starts to leave our bodies, we will want another. Not in an hour, not in a day, not next time we go out or next time we have a drink, but now. And if we don't let ourselves have one we will fantasize about it, we will anticipate it, we will obsess about it—in other words, we will crave it. And while we crave it we will disengage from life and we will be miserable as all our focus is on an internal and unpleasant conflict.

This is one of the great and horrible truths about smoking: most of the cigarettes we smoke we don't even particularly enjoy, but this does not mean we can cut them out because we are just as miserable without them as we are when we can't have the ones that we believe are genuinely enjoyable. This is the reality of smoking: it's all negative. Even the ones we believe we enjoy are negative because the so-called enjoyment is just a matter of removing the unpleasant feeling we get when the last dose wears off. But even if that enjoyment were genuine, it's missing from the majority of cigarettes we smoke.

So cutting down is never the perfect solution we think it is. Remember, smoking is not habit, it is addiction. You will never get into the habit of smoking less than you do now. You may, through circumstances and/or willpower, force yourself to smoke less, but it will never feel normal and natural to do so, it will never become habit. Indeed, many people find that their obsession with smoking increases dramatically when they cut down. They may smoke less, but they are thinking about smoking an awful lot more. Whereas when they were smoking whenever they liked, the cigarette may have been smoldering away in their hand or mouth largely unnoticed while they got on with their lives. But as soon as they try to cut down, they spend most of their waking life thinking about that next cigarette. They go through their lives almost constantly in the fantasy stage of craving, constantly thinking about their next smoke. It's in this stage that a lot of people think they have memory or concentration problems. You may walk into a room to get something but suddenly have no idea what you were supposed to get, or keep flicking that switch when the power is off. But in fact, it's not a memory problem, it's that 70 percent of your attention and mental bandwidth are taken up with thinking about that next cigarette.

So it cutting down possible? Theoretically, yes. After all, no one forces you to smoke, and if you want to smoke less, then there is nothing physically preventing you from doing so. But practically, it is fraught with difficulties. However, the main problem is not whether cutting down is possible, but whether it is worthwhile, and this is where the real issue lies. When we think about cutting down we think about smoking only those really enjoyable cigarettes, and going on our merry way when we're not smoking. But, the reality is that we don't merrily continue with our lives after smoking them, instead we crave and obsess when we aren't smoking. Therefore the reality of cutting down is not the ideal solution we hoped it would be.

Have you ever been in a situation where you could smoke as much as you wanted, and ended up smoking when you didn't even want to? When you ended up lighting a cigarette wondering why on earth you were doing so, yet not able to stop? That can feel totally irrational, but there is a perfectly rational explanation for it.

The longer we've smoked, the more attuned we become to feeling the withdrawal. It doesn't take long before we notice the withdrawal almost as soon as the last dose ends. However, what we also become attuned to is the craving. We realize (on a subconscious level) that if we think about having a cigarette and we don't have one we can experience an unpleasant internal mental tantrum. When you are in a situation where you can smoke as much as you like, the thought of a cigarette is almost constantly on your mind. Your subconscious very quickly learns that it's far easier to just light the wretched thing and short-circuit the craving process, instead of sitting there for even a few minutes while it goes on.

This is the natural conclusion of smoking: chain-smoking. To relieve the withdrawal and avoid the craving instead of having to suffer it.

So much for cutting down, but what about substitutes? When we quit smoking we feel like something is missing, there's a feeling that our little regular reward, our little treat, out little escape from the daily grind is gone. The temptation is to look for something to fill that gap.

When thinking about substitutes, what we need to bear in mind is that a lot of that feeling of something missing is actually just the withdrawal; it goes away within a few days. But there's also a nasty trap you can fall into if you aren't careful.

We often smoke when we are stressed, when something bad happens. This needn't be something major, it could just be one of those little things that happen every day to everyone and that are a part of human life: an argument with a friend, a difficult assignment, a problem at work, or what have you. When this happens, we have a smoke to take the edge off of things before getting on and dealing with them. We become very accustomed to consuming something to change how we feel. When cigarettes are off the menu there is a marked tendency to just reach for the next thing to consume to change how you feel—caffeine, sugar, alcohol, snacks. Consuming something to change how you feel becomes a subconscious reaction to any kind of stress.

Some of these things may well be far less damaging than smoking, but all of them are frustrating, ultimately unpleasant, and (most importantly) they don't work, and by this I mean they take far more then they give. Take food as an example. If you are hungry and eat a good meal, you will feel loads better. It is genuinely enjoyable. It will improve your mood. So you can easily fall into the habit of eating whenever you need a lift. But if you aren't hungry, if you are full, and you keep stuffing your face with chocolate or chips or whatever, you aren't going to feel better, you're going to feel worse. You're going to feel uncomfortable, bloated, fat, and miserable. You're going to put on weight. You won't even enjoy it when you're eating. Substituting has two effects: first, it stops you living your best, most enjoyable life. Second, it makes you more likely to end up smoking again. After all, if you quit and you find that your life is full of frustration and misery, aren't you far more likely to just throw in the towel and go back to the devil you know? If you are constantly overeating and finding yourself feeling uncomfortable, overweight, and unhappy, and you think back on those happy, carefree days when you were smoking (thanks also to the warping effects of FAB and ambition) and you will be far more likely to end up smoking again.

This mechanism feeds into the myth of the addictive personality, that belief that some people are just prone to get addicted to things whereas others aren't. Many people quit one thing only to move on to the next; they seem to limp from one addiction to another. But this is not a personality issue, it's a coping mechanism. When you have a bad day, do you consume something to change how you feel? Do you smoke a cigarette, have a drink, or gobble a load of refined sugar or fatty red meat? Or do you read a book, talk to a friend, go for a walk, a run, a swim, to the gym, watch a film or show, or lose yourself in a hobby? How do you deal with stress?

Life for everyone—non-smokers, smokers, vapers, dippers, everyone—has ups and downs. This is a simple fact. No one is happy all the time. In Western society we have become very conditioned to expect to be happy all the time. We may see it as our right. This isn't necessarily a bad thing, after all, who wants to be miserable? The problem is that instead of doing something healthy and productive to alleviate stress, we have a marked tendency to consume something to change how we feel. There isn't any such thing as an addictive personality.

There was a period when it was thought that genetics could explain addiction. Although there may be links between certain genetics and addiction to certain drugs, genetics does not dictate addiction. Professor David Nutt, in his book *Drugs Without the Hot Air*, describes it this way:

"While genes may predict vulnerabilities, not having those genes certainly doesn't make us invulnerable. This is particularly true in terms of vulnerability to addiction, as it's a learned behaviour that requires voluntary repetition in order to become habitual."

Some people may be physically stronger, physically fitter, and be better able to tolerate larger doses of a poison such as nicotine, alcohol, and other drugs and consequently will find taking these poisons easier and will be able to consume more of them. So, if you look at a population of smokers or other addicts, you will most certainly find that people with a certain genetic code will be overrepresented in that population. But people without that genetic code will still be in the addicted population, and there will always be people *with* that genetic code who aren't addicted. It is behavior, not genetics, that is the problem, and behavior is learned and can be changed.

So there are no addictive personalities, but there are two ways you can react when the bad times come. You can rely on substances in an attempt to solve your problems, or you can decide to adopt healthier coping mechanisms.

This brings us to nicotine replacement therapy, or NRT, which is essentially taking nicotine by means other than tobacco to aid quitting. The idea behind it is that smoking is made up of part habit, part chemical dependency. So, you put on a nicotine patch or chew nicotine gum while you get used to not smoking, then slowly wean yourself off of the nicotine. And even if you aren't successful in cutting out the nicotine, then better to chew gum or stick on a patch than smoke, as it is less harmful for you. It is thought to be a useful tool in quitting.

The problem with NRT is that it is founded on a false premise: that smoking has anything to do with habit. As we've noted earlier, smoking isn't habit but drug addiction. And as we've already covered, addiction and habit are very different things. If you are in any doubt about this, get some nicotine-free cigarettes and see how habitually you end up smoking those. People smoke because they have an unpleasant feeling building up that they want to get rid of, which has nothing to do with habit.

So, if the issue is purely one of addiction to a particular drug, what are we trying to do to deal with it? Well, that's fairly simple, we want to no longer be addicted to it. Do you think you achieve this by taking the drug in a different form, or by cutting it out entirely? In fact, there are other reasons why taking a drug to kick a drug isn't the best way to proceed.

As we've discussed previously, your brain interprets the withdrawal as "I want a cigarette." We've also covered how your brain is continually seeking to counter the stimulating effects of the nicotine. So to never, ever have the withdrawal you would need to keep an ever-increasing flow of nicotine into your bloodstream. This has practical as well as health implications, and in any event doesn't address the main issue, which is that our goal here is to no longer be addicted to nicotine.

But what about using NRT to slowly wean yourself off of nicotine? The problem with this is that the brain interprets the withdrawal as "I need a smoke." NRT elongates the withdrawal phase; by keeping up the supply of nicotine to the body, you keep the withdrawal alive, which in turn keeps the physical desire to smoke going for far longer.

The great pleasure in not smoking is to stop interfering with the delicate chemical balance of your mind. When you do this you go through a few days or weeks when your brain needs to readjust to no longer having to recalibrate in reaction to a regular dose of an alien stimulant (by alien, I mean that it comes from outside the body and is not one of the naturally occurring chemicals that the brain creates and excretes). When you do this you feel more confident, more resilient, better able to cope with life that you ever did when you were a nicotine addict, even when you were enjoying that first smoke or vape hit of the day. And the best part is that you feel like that all the time, not just for a few precious moments every day. When you stop regularly elevating your heart with a chemical substance, you have more energy and your fitness levels quickly recover, and this in turn has a massive positive impact on your mental resilience and thus your quality of life.

Obviously this is your life, your decision, and your relationship with nicotine. For me, personally, I wanted to get to this stage as soon as possible. I didn't want to lengthen it by a single moment. I wanted to be free as soon as possible.

ENGAGEMENT POINT

How do you think it would be best to quit, cold turkey or by using NRT? Think about what the withdrawal is and why it's a problem. If you do a few internet searches on nicotine withdrawal you'll see that most of them aren't too awful: inability to concentrate, irritability, possibly headaches. Physically, it's not really any worse than having a cold for a few days, leaving you a bit spaced-out and not really with it. In fact the biggest and most problematic withdrawal symptoms are the cravings. We've dealt with cravings; they are a conscious thought process that can be disrupted and avoided. The physical withdrawal doesn't cause the craving. It can put the thought of a cigarette into your mind, but it's what you do with that thought that determines whether it turns into a craving.

14.

Smoking Helps Me Relax

We've already covered in some depth how smoking doesn't relieve stress, but the idea of kicking back with a smoke, of taking a few minutes out of a hectic day to just sit back and chill with a smoke or a vape, is a very hard concept to rid yourself of. Let's delve into this in a bit more detail.

First of all, what is relaxation? There are two elements to it, the physical and the mental. Physically, we usually stop moving, sit down, and have a bit of physical rest. Second, there is what happens mentally.

The second element is essentially emptying your mind a bit, letting go of all the things that have been stressing you during the day: kids, work, college, friends, family. It's about just sitting back and letting go of all those irritants. This is what meditation is; it's about emptying your mind of conscious thought, that is, forgetting all the things that are making you uptight and irritated.

This is how smoking or vaping can feel like it's helping us relax. Let's say you are in college, or in the office, and you decide that it's all getting a bit too much and want to take a few minutes out and have a smoke. First let's remember that gone are the days when you could just light up at your desk. You have to physically go outside the building, usually to a designated smoking area. You sit down or stand, light up, and spend a few minutes just staring at the horizon (or your phone screen) and enjoy relieving that withdrawal. Then you go back in, feeling almost like you've had a mini holiday, a chance to take some time out to relax, then you're back, ready to continue on with the day.

Another time might be when you've actually finished for the day. You're walking to the train station or your car or the bus and you have a smoke. Or even when you get home, you sit down and have a smoke and that's what allows you to rid your mind of all the stresses and strains of the day, to transition from work to relaxation. So again, let's drag this aspect out of our subconscious, shine the light of reason on it, break it down into its various parts, and see if we can't understand it in a bit more detail.

As we've touched on, relaxing is about physically stopping, sometimes even removing yourself from a situation, but more importantly, it requires emptying your mind of whatever is causing you to be stressed. If you are trying to relax at the end of the working day, it's about slowly leaving thoughts of work behind, and moving toward thoughts about your free time, getting home and having a meal, working out, relaxing in front of the TV, reading a book, meeting friends, and so on.

People who aren't addicted to nicotine do this naturally. They walk out of the office, or walk out of class, or close down their laptop at the end of the day. They stop work and start doing the relaxing things that they do in the evening. They turn their minds to the evening meal, meeting friends, their favorite show on TV, the book they are reading, time with their partner, time with their family, a game, a magazine, or social media. As they do this, their mind turns from work to play and they slowly calm down and relax into the evening.

However, if you are addicted to nicotine, you won't be able to relax into the evening unless you have a dose of it. The nicotine withdrawal will be there, be it severe or not so severe, but it will be there. You will think about a cigarette, you will start to fantasize about it and anticipate it, in other words you will start to crave it. You won't be able to relax into the evening, to start thinking about your evening meal or your book or the TV or whatever it is you do to relax, because your mind will be taken up with thinking about smoking. When you then have your cigarette, your dose of nicotine, you will no longer be obsessing about that smoke, you will be able then to concentrate on other things, which is that transition from work to play.

Addiction is a prison, but a prison where the drug is the jailer, the gatekeeper. It keeps you locked up in a prison of anxiety and mental frailty, but if you're nice to it, if you bow to it and do as it bids you, it sometimes lets you out to have a taste of what life would be like if you were free. When you smoke or vape, that nicotine jailer opens the prison door for a few minutes to let you out. You're not totally free, you have a shackle that's on a chain attached to a winch and the second you get out that winch starts slowly, inexorably dragging you back again. You are never truly free, but you get to have a little taste of freedom. You're locked up in this prison, but every time you take a dose of your drug, every time you destroy yourself a little more with a poison, your jailer lets you out on this extended leash. But it's on an automated winch system, and although you may have a hundred or two hundred yards of leash, the winding process starts the second you're released.

This is true of every aspect of smoking, and is particularly easy to see when relaxing. If you don't smoke, you just transition from work to play, it becomes natural. The walk, drive, or train journey from the office, or, if you're home working, the act of turning off your laptop and walking away from your work area becomes your transition. But if you smoke you can't make this shift while you're being distracted by the withdrawal and the thought of smoking. Your addiction to nicotine prevents you from making this transition naturally. So you have a smoke, you take your little dose of nicotine, you kill yourself a little more, and as a reward for being a good inmate and doing what you're told, your jailer lets you out for a few minutes to experience a life of freedom; in this case to make the transition from work to relaxation like non-smokers the world over do all the time.

The jailer is strong and so is the prison, but it's not stronger than you. Regular doses of nicotine make you weak, mentally as well as physically. In your natural state the jailer and the prison are no match for you; you could break out of it easily. But regular doses of nicotine make you weak and unable to break free. Because your jailer lets you out when you take a dose, you end up being fooled into thinking that the jailer is a friend—after all, it's kind to you and lets you sample freedom. Worse than this, you don't even fully realize that the prison exists. You assume that everyone lives in a prison, but that those who don't pay homage to the nicotine jailer don't get to sample this freedom. Those poor non-smokers don't know what they're missing, they don't get to kick back and let the stresses and strains of everyday life wash over them, they don't get to experience freedom.

What we don't appreciate is that non-smokers aren't in a prison to begin with. What we also lose sight of is that the only way to leave that prison, always and forever, is to stop smoking. The prison is weak and so is the jailer, the only reason it can hold us is because we are fooled into playing along, we acquiesce, and because the jailer gives us freedom we think of it as a friend. As soon as we stop taking the poison, the very second we finish our final dose of it, our strength will start to return. We will break free of the leash and walk away, never to return. You will experience a relaxation that you won't have experienced since you started smoking. Even while smoking you have additional stress factors caused by your nicotine addiction that aren't dispelled when you are smoking—the cognitive dissonance, the worry about health, the costs, and so on. These are like dark shadows at the back of your mind that you try to forget about but that never truly go away, until the day you finally quit.

15.

Defining Addiction

Some people struggle to accept that their smoking or vaping behavior is all about addiction to nicotine. What you sometimes hear from people is, "I don't smoke because I'm addicted, I smoke because I enjoy it." There is a lot of misunderstanding about the line between addiction and enjoyment. Addicts, all addicts, enjoy relieving the withdrawal. They may hate themselves for having to do it, they may be disgusted and horrified at themselves, but that moment when the drug kicks in is one of pure, unadulterated pleasure. Why? Because it takes away all the horror, the fear, the misery, the terror, and leaves them once again feeling calm, content, relaxed, and able to cope with life. In other words it allows them, for a few moments, to feel how they would feel had they never taken the drug in the first place.

So what is the difference between doing something enjoyable and doing something because we are addicted to it? The word *addiction* is used so much these days. Not just for drugs but for other things as well. Sex, gambling, food. How do you know if you are doing something because you're addicted to it, or because you genuinely enjoy it?

The first thing we need to bear in mind is that there is a gray area between enjoyment and addiction. It's not just the case that one ends and the other begins. As I've mentioned, relieving the withdrawal from a drug is enjoyable. For all the downsides there are with nicotine, the one thing it has in its favor is that even for the most physically addicted person, the withdrawal is not on the same level as something like heroin. It may be unpleasant but it amounts to a few days of feeling unfocused, out of sorts, slightly woolly-headed and maybe tired and headachy. You don't get the screaming, shaking, life-threatening horrors that you can get when you try to stop taking other drugs.

This is good on the one hand because it means the physical side of quitting is usually quite manageable for most people and medical intervention is not necessary. But it can cause problems for other reasons. Because the withdrawal is quite subtle when compared to other drugs, it can make it hard for people to accept that they are addicted and that the pleasure that they experience comes from relieving the withdrawal and nothing else. All most smokers or vapers really know is that breathing in smoke and vapor is enjoyable, that the taste and the feeling of the smoke going into their lungs feels good, so they want to keep doing it. In fact it's only over the last few decades that people even realized that smoking was all about nicotine addiction. The general view used to be that smoking was an enjoyable thing to do, and nicotine addiction was an unwanted side effect that affected some people who smoked, like lung cancer and crushing heart attacks in middle age. The big tobacco companies at one point invested a lot in nicotine-free cigarettes in an attempt to produce a "clean" cigarette, but what they very quickly learned was that a cigarette without nicotine was totally pointless, and that the entire point of smoking was to get a dose of nicotine. However, for some people this myth remains.

Because the word *addiction* has so many different meanings, psychiatrists prefer the term *substance use disorder*. Substance use disorders are classified according to certain characteristic features that fall into three categories: abuse, dependence, and craving.

Abuse is characterized by significant negative consequences to the addicted. These can be health consequences, relational consequences, and consequences from no longer doing what you should be doing—like going to work in the morning. Most people are aware of the health consequences for smoking, vaping, and dipping (we talk about the health consequences of vaping later in the book), like lung cancer, middle-aged heart attacks, strokes, mouth cancer, throat cancer, and more. We try to hide away from these serious consequences as best we can, and we make our thinly veiled excuses as to why they don't apply to us, but the reality is that nicotine is a poison, it kills living things, and your lungs are not designed to breathe it in on a regular basis. You are going to be hard-pressed to convince yourself or any other rational human being that it's anything other than harmful for you.

Dependence happens when the addict depends on the drug psychologically and sometimes physically. Dependence is characterized by tolerance, when you need to consume more of the drug to get the same effect, and withdrawal, when you have unpleasant psychological or physical symptoms when you stop taking the drug. Both occur when your body and brain have changed to compensate for the chronic presence of the drug.

We have discussed craving in considerable detail—it is an extremely strong, seemingly illogical desire to use the drug. Cravings can contradict your feelings, meaning you may consciously desire to not smoke, but you still have an intense craving, or desire, to keep doing it.

For simplicity, let's define *addiction* this way: doing something on a regular basis that part of you does not want to be doing. Or doing something more often than you would like to be doing, yet being unable to easily stop or cut back. Basically, it's having two competing priorities, wanting to do both more and less of something at the same time.

It is also the case, with physical addiction, that there is the physiological side. In this case I think the definition of addiction is far easier: it's taking a drug to feel normal, or at least closer to normal than you feel before you take it. Essentially it's regularly taking a drug to relieve the withdrawal pangs created by the last dose of the drug.

As the cycle continues, the feeling of dependence becomes greater, and we begin to believe that smoking is the most important thing in our lives. In a way it *is* the most important thing, because we can't enjoy our lives without it. The withdrawal kicks in, then the craving, at which stage we totally disengage in life and become entirely taken up with an unpleasant internal obsession. Just as bad food would taste amazing if we were starving, our perception of smoking is altered. It becomes increasingly valuable, increasingly crucial.

Eventually, as we become increasingly attuned to both the withdrawal and the craving, we increase our intake, which increases the damage to our mental and physical health. The illusion of enjoyment or relief becomes almost nonexistent. We may now start to listen to family and friends or pay attention to the small, cautionary voice inside our heads. We wonder if we should cut back or quit. Yet we've been conditioned to believe cutting back or quitting is difficult, so we sadly begin to prepare for an uphill battle.

We try to abstain, but our subconscious and conscious mind still believe we are receiving enjoyment or relief from smoking. Think of that ever-narrowing causeway—the narrower it is, the more desperate we are to extend its width. We feel miserable and depressed when we are trying to quit. We believe we are sacrificing something that has become important. Since we still see people who appear to be happily smoking, we feel like we are missing out. Ultimately, our actual experiences confirm our belief that it is hard, if not impossible, to stop smoking.

The longer we deprive ourselves, the greater the illusion of pleasure when we finally give in. Why? Through abstinence, the feeling of misery has grown. Not only does abstinence cause the withdrawal to intensify, but it can also cause the cravings to continue. The longer we suffer pain or discomfort, the greater the relief when we finally relieve it. We translate this relief into pleasure when we finally give in and smoke. In this cycle of addiction, both the misery of abstinence and the pleasure of surrender are real and intense.

16.

Life as a Nicotine Addict

One of the problems with smoking and vaping is that we don't actually appreciate their immediate, short-term disadvantages, the most obvious of which is how lethargic and heavy smoking makes us feel. When I was smoking in my late teens I had my resting heart rate measured by a friend who was studying physical education in college. I'd just had a cigarette. My heart rate was 90. Now I'm forty-six years old. According to my fitness tracker (for those of you not familiar with these, they are essentially watches that track your heart rate, steps, and sleep) my average resting heart rate is 55; it drops to around 42 most nights when I'm asleep. When I go for a run my heart rate goes up to around 100.

Think about the implications of this. Everyone has a maximum heart rate (calculated by subtracting your age from 220). The higher your heart rate goes up, the more your brain tells you to slow down, to stop, to rest. When it goes up a little bit you're fine, the desire to stop is almost imperceptible; it's more like a mild preference than a desire. Everyone is different, but I am happy to run, with my heart rate at 90, for as long as I can get away with (I usually do about forty minutes and I enjoy it; it causes me no discomfort at all). But what I don't like, and never have, is sprint training, when you suddenly go all out and run as fast as you can for a period. I find that unpleasant. That's when my heart rate goes up beyond 100.

Again, these days when my heart rate reaches more than 100, I am uncomfortable and want to slow down and stop. However, in my late teens, right after smoking a cigarette, my heart rate was 90. I could probably stand up, and maybe take a walk, and that would be my limit. Now, in my mid-forties, I can run for forty minutes to get the same effect.

What you need to bear in mind is how this affects your quality of life on a day-to-day basis. As far as my heart rate goes, I've got fuel in the tank every day now. I've got energy, I feel light and energetic; most of the time, anyway. This has a knock-on effect on how I feel mentally. Remember, ill health makes you feel timid and unadventurous, and when you're bristling with energy you feel confident and capable. This isn't to say that I don't have bad days, of course I do, everyone does. But the smaller things have less chance of derailing me so I have fewer truly bad days, and I tend to be able to bounce back after only a day or so, instead of being derailed for days at a time.

The belief that the health effects of smoking or vaping are hit or miss (for example, that you may get a killer disease, but if you don't get one, you get away totally) is a dangerous and incorrect one. Every dose of nicotine is destroying you, not only in the long term but also destroying your quality of life right here and now.

As smokers, we don't realize that our chronic exhaustion is related to continuously poisoning our bodies, still less do we appreciate the huge effect that this has on our confidence, mental resilience, and quality of life generally. These are immediate, unpleasant, and very real and noticeable effects of smoking and vaping.

ENGAGEMENT POINT

Heart rate is measured in bpm (beats per minute), the number of times your heart beats in one minute. When you wake up tomorrow, measure your heart rate before you even get out of bed. To do this:

1. Hold out one of your hands, with the palm up.
2. Put your index and middle fingers of your other hand on the inside of your wrist underneath the base of your thumb.
3. Press down gently until you can feel your pulse. You may need to move your finger around to find it.
4. Time one minute, and count how many times your heart beats in that minute.

Make a note of this count.

Measure again directly after your first smoke or vape hit of the day. Compare the two readings.

Think of the difference this makes in how you feel. This variation in heart rate is an actual, measurable indicator of how light, energetic, and positive you feel—or don't feel.

Really start to notice this heavy, lethargic feeling. Start to associate it with smoking or vaping.

17.

Smoking Helps Me Concentrate

The idea that smoking enhances concentration is a big thing for many people, one of the so-called central truths that make it hard to stop. After all, if you have something difficult to concentrate on, it's impossible not to want that extra boost smoking or vaping gives you, right? But what actually is concentration? And how can breathing in an addictive drug help with it? As ever, it helps to actually drill down into these questions, to get under the skin of them to really understand what's going on here so we can see if our core beliefs are correct.

Concentration essentially occurs when you focus all your attention on something. So how do you do this? For most people it actually has to do with removing distractions. Most people these days work in open-plan offices, so if they have something difficult to do they may take themselves away to a quiet area. If you have a challenging task to accomplish at home you may try to find somewhere quiet, turn the music off, give the kids something to keep them occupied, and put away your cell phone so it's not the usual drain on your attention.

When you have removed all the possible distractions, you can move forward with the job at hand.

The trouble is that the smoker, dipper, or vaper has two additional distractions, one large, one not so large. The not-so-large one is the physical withdrawal from nicotine. The large one is the craving process. After all, how are we going to concentrate on this difficult job we have to do if 90 percent of our attention is being taken up with an unpleasant internal dialogue about smoking?

But hang on, why am I saying that the physical withdrawal isn't the large part? Nicotine is a stimulant, right? It's going to help you concentrate? This brings us to a slightly more intricate part of concentration: it's not always possible to remove all distractions, and if you can't, you don't just give up, you get on with the job at hand anyway.

Let's say you are at work in your open-plan office and there's a lot of talking going on among your colleagues, but you've got something you have to finish in an hour. It's a busy day, there's nowhere quiet you can go. You just keep working, right? You don't quit your job just because there are people talking near you. Or say you are at home and the kids have got the TV on, which is making noise, but if you turn if off they're going to end up doing something else even noisier. Or your neighbor's car alarm is going off, or there's construction going on nearby.

Imagine trying to coordinate and direct a battle with thousands of people under your command. Imagine the chaos and noise of battle. Does that stop military leaders from doing their job? Did Eisenhower or Wellington ever throw their hands in the air and say, "This is intolerable. I can't concentrate with all this noise going on, I'm giving up!"

The fact is that we are capable of ignoring distractions when we need to. The human brain is incredibly good at tuning distractions out and concentrating on one single part of something that is made up of dozens of parts.

Have you ever sat in a really noisy restaurant or bar with a friend?

You are easily able to sit and talk to them and listen to what they say. But when they go to the restroom, suddenly you can hear the conversations of the people all around you. There may be four or five conversations going on within earshot of you. At the end of the evening you will remember what your friend was saying to you and won't have a clue about any of the other conversations when you and your friend were talking because *you weren't listening*. You phased them out. Although the people around you may have been almost as loud as your friend, you were able to ignore them and concentrate on what your friend was saying.

Have you ever been to a picture gallery and looked at one of those massive panorama landscape pictures? Of one of those paintings, for example, of a Civil War battle? You can be standing six feet away, looking at this huge picture with so much detail going on in it. Then you suddenly focus in on one small bit—a bird in a tree, a soldier holding a flag, a particular fallen combatant—and suddenly the rest of the picture ceases to exist as you concentrate on that one small part.

The fact is that the human brain is incredibly good at blocking out what it doesn't want to be distracted with, so we are able to concentrate, to focus our attention on something, even with some quite severe distractions. So the problem is not that things are distracting per se. The real issue is whether our mind is able to ignore the distraction. So what decides this?

The main differentiator is whether we can do something about the distraction. Imagine you're at home and you have something you really need to concentrate on and it needs to be done in the next hour. You sit down and then you hear a dripping noise. There's a tap dripping in the bathroom next door—someone didn't bother to turn it off properly. All you have to do is get up, tighten that tap, and crack on. Chances are you wouldn't be able to concentrate until you did this. Every time you heard that dripping sound you would think, "I need to get up and sort that out." And that thought alone will distract you; after all, if you are thinking about turning a tap off you aren't thinking about or concentrating 100 percent on the job you need to do.

But let's say the tap is dripping because it's broken. You can't fix it, let's say either you're missing a part or you don't know how to fix it, so you've arranged for someone to come out and fix it or you've ordered the part, but it can't be done until tomorrow. So what do you do? You ignore it. You've got no choice, after all. You hear the drip, but it doesn't trigger the "I really need to do something about that" thought because you can't do anything about it right now. And because you don't have this thought, it can't distract you from the job at hand. Think about that military leader, planning out the battle even as the bullets and bombs fly past. This extreme is what we are capable of, so do you really think the drip of a tap is going to derail you?

That's what we do when we need to concentrate; we remove the distractions we can and we put up with what we can't and we get on with what we need to do. So there are two parts: the physical distraction and our reaction to it.

So what's this got to do with the withdrawal being the small part and the craving being the large part when it comes to smoking and concentration? As mentioned previously, the physical withdrawal from nicotine is unpleasant, but it is mild when compared with other drugs. Even the very heaviest long-term smokers don't need medical intervention to see them safely through the withdrawal. It amounts to feeling unfocused and out of sorts, as noted earlier. Like caffeine withdrawal there may be some headaches, but that's about it. This physical withdrawal may be the distraction, but the craving process is our reaction to it.

If we need to concentrate in a situation where smoking is possible, then that alone will dictate that we cannot concentrate *without* smoking, because the possibility of being able to smoke will start the craving process. Suddenly, 90 percent of our attention will be focused inward on that unpleasant internal argument. Of course we won't be able to concentrate.

However, when we can't smoke and the possibility of smoking is off the table, then the craving doesn't kick in. Smoking becomes one of those distractions that, as we can't do anything about, we just ignore and keep going.

You don't believe me? You don't think you're able to concentrate on something difficult without a smoke even if the abstinence is forced upon you? If you genuinely think you can't concentrate without smoking whether you are allowed to smoke or not, you have a great example of the confirmation bias that we were talking about at the beginning of the book. Again, confirmation bias is the idea that we form a belief (in this case, the belief is that we need to smoke to concentrate) and we accept all the experiences we have that confirm it (like all the times we've sat down and smoked or vaped, then been able to really concentrate on something) and we disregard from our minds all the experiences that totally contradict that belief.

Many smoker and vapers genuinely believe that smoking or vaping helps them to concentrate, and that they cannot concentrate without their smoke or vape. But then they may remember many occasions when they were able to concentrate just fine when the abstinence from nicotine was forced on them. Maybe they took a test or an exam, or worked or read while on an airplane, a train, or any form of public transport where smoking is not allowed. Maybe they got caught up in something in their non-smoking office and were so enmeshed in it that they not only didn't think about smoking, but even ended up missing their usual smoke or vape break. They may have been at the theater or cinema and because the option to smoke wasn't available, didn't spend any time fantasizing about it. Even if the thought of a cigarette had crossed their mind briefly, the impossibility of smoking meant that the anticipation stage of the craving did not kick in. They were able to avoid a full-blown craving.

Some people will tell you that smoking does actually aid concentration because it is a stimulant and that it will boost alertness and recall ability. However, what they miss is that the brain compensates for the stimulating effect of the nicotine (which we covered in detail in chapter 4) so that pretty soon you smoke just to feel normal. So yes, if you are in the nicotine withdrawal phase and you have a cigarette, you may have some increased mental ability, but this will not be over and above the mental ability you would have had you never smoked. The withdrawal causes brain fog, and the next smoke relieves it. Net gain? *Zilch!* And after a few days, if you quit, the withdrawal disappears totally, forever, never to return, which means you are in a heightened mental state *constantly*. You will never again need a cigarette to get you back to where you ought to be.

So smoking doesn't help us concentrate, it just removes that ability, then partially restores it. It's the same old mechanism, the same as every other aspect of smoking, vaping, and dipping. No gain, just losing something then getting a bit of it back. It's me again, giving you that $100, while in the background your bank balance just keeps on shrinking.

18.

Is Smoking Social?

Years ago, when smoking was still allowed in most public places, it was seen as a social thing to do. When people met for the first time they would produce their cigarettes, offer them around, and try each other's. It was seen as an icebreaker. But again, it is useful to delve into this idea a bit further. We use a lot of words so often without every really stopping to think about their meaning and implications. First, let's look at socializing, what it entails, and why we do it.

Socializing is when we come together with other human beings and interact with them. It is a part of human existence, whether we do it through our work or on our free time. Hanging out with friends, going to business meetings, and spending time with the family are all examples of socializing. Human beings are social animals; most of us need some form of social interaction. Most people have heard of endorphins: natural chemicals released by the brain that make us feel good. We get them when we eat a healthy meal, when we exercise, when we have sex, and when we socialize.

Of course, we are all different; some people are more extroverted whereas others are more introverted. Extroverted means you love social engagement, you thrive on it. Introverted means the opposite, you dislike social occasions and try to avoid them as much as possible.

Like most things when it comes to human beings, people are rarely one extreme or the other. Even very extroverted people are likely to need some quiet, alone time at some point, and even very introverted people like to enjoy some social interaction, even if it is just with one or two people that they know very well and are comfortable with.

The key to getting endorphins when we socialize is to be relaxed and happy. The problem is that we're all products of our society, we all care (to a greater or lesser degree) what other people think of us. So the usual dynamic is that we go out to a social occasion and, for the first part, we feel slightly anxious and uncomfortable. We worry about what people will think of us, what we'll say, how we will come across. We're not fully relaxed. So we don't get this endorphin high immediately. However, as we start to relax and start to talk to people, as we think more about the topics of conversation and less about what we look like and how we come across, we start to ease into the social event. Remember, your brain can only think of a finite number of things at any one time. When you turn up at a social event your thoughts tend to circle around *What will I say? How do I look? Who do I know? What if I end up standing alone?* But if you get into a conversation that interests and engages you, you will end up concentrating more and more on the topic of conversation. When you end up fully engaged in the social interaction, there's no room in your brain to worry about how you look or whether you'll say something stupid. Because you're not worrying about the occasion, and you're just socializing, the endorphins start to flow. It's a subtle feeling, but a good one. And the quality of the conversation is important—the interaction needs to be interesting and stimulating.

If you are very introverted, it will take you longer to relax into the evening than someone who is very extroverted, but we all get there in the end. This is what an icebreaker is—something that encourages that early interaction, that gets the conversation flowing so that people can relax into the event and start to enjoy themselves.

This is where smoking once did have an element of sociality, however small. When people met for the first time they would bring out their smokes, offer them around, talk about them—which brands they smoked, which they didn't like—and it would be an icebreaker.

Today, people just use other topics of conversation to break the ice, they talk about their jobs, their neighborhoods, their families, their friends, sports, in fact all the things that genuinely define them, instead of which particular brand of poison they are compelled to murder themselves with. Because if you smoke, and you meet someone who smokes, and you spend the first twenty minutes talking about smoking, you still know nothing about them. After you've covered smoking you then go on to real topics, and you may find you're totally incompatible. Maybe they then launch into a vitriolic political rant that you find deeply offensive, or a really boring story that you can't wait to stop listening to. So it turns out that even this so-called benefit of smoking as an icebreaker is false. There are a hundred other ways to break the ice at a social event, and talking about a drug addiction is never a good start because it stops you from really finding out about the person you are talking with, and stops you sharing your true self with them, which is the real heart of social interaction.

The impact of smoking or vaping on social events doesn't just end here, of course. If you are a smoker or a vaper you have an automatic additional barrier that can stop you from relaxing into the evening: the nicotine withdrawal and craving cycle. If you've got a bit of brain fog, then relaxing into the event is going to be a bit harder, and if you aren't concentrating on the conversation at all and instead have all your attention taken up with a torturous internal debate, then relaxing is impossible. So what do you do? You go and have a smoke or a vape hit, then you're back, ready to do what the non-smoker was doing all along—settling into and enjoying the event.

It's the old dynamic. Smoking never did help, it just stopped you from experiencing something and then it let you have it back. As long as you keep sacrificing at its altar, it keeps granting you bits of your life back. There you are, free from your prison again, but on a leash attached to a winch that is slowly, inexorably, dragging you back. It certainly doesn't sound like a fair deal.

At social events these days, if you want to vape or smoke, you usually have to go outside the home or venue. This can lead people to genuinely believe that there is an additional social aspect to smoking and vaping. It's not just at social events, but also at work. People who regularly go out to vape or smoke often form new friendships with others who do the same. The main event is going on indoors, while a mini social event is happening outside as people go out to smoke and vape. A lot of people think that these mini outdoor social events are important and they will miss them when they quit. They worry about missing out on this special club, but it never seems to dawn on them what social interactions they might be missing out on that are going on indoors while they are outdoors. If you are at a social event, you're socializing whether you are inside or outside. When you're socializing indoors you can't be socializing outdoors, and vice versa. There is no net gain or loss.

But in fact the smoker or vaper does have it worse off. At most social events (if they are big enough) we cycle through different people as the evening wears on. Even at smaller events we may start mainly speaking to the person on our right, then our left, then we go to the bar or restroom and end up sitting next to someone else. Every time we move we have to go through a little mini icebreaking process before we relax back into the conversation. These are small disruptions to the socializing process. The smoker or vaper adds in disruptions throughout the event as they constantly have to leave to feed their addiction. But it doesn't end there.

Most smokers don't chain-smoke, particularly not at social occasions if they have to smoke outside. As soon as the smoker or vaper stops the intake of nicotine, the withdrawal starts to build. Slowly at first, but ever increasing in intensity. How attuned they are to the withdrawal dictates how quickly they will start to notice this withdrawal after the last dose wears off. However, when they do notice the withdrawal (either consciously or subconsciously) the craving process will start. A little voice will start up at the back of their mind, saying how nice it would be to have a smoke. As the withdrawal increases so will the thought of the cigarette, and the craving starts to kick in. You may be taking to someone you find genuinely interesting and engaging, you may be 100 percent focused on the conversation. But when that little thought enters your mind you're suddenly only 95 percent focusing on the conversation because 5 percent of your mind is thinking about a smoke, and as the withdrawal and craving increases your mind is taken up more and more with smoking and less and less with the conversation that you should be enjoying and engaging in. Pretty soon you aren't listening to a word that other person is saying, all you're thinking now is "Will you please shut up for just two seconds so I can disengage and get out for a smoke!"

When you smoke at social events, the pleasure you take in the event is determined mainly by how often you can relieve your withdrawal, and to a lesser degree by the actual socializing. The socializing always plays second fiddle to the smoking. Smoking or vaping interrupts the natural run of social occasions. One of the great unexpected pleasures of quitting nicotine is to go back to normal socializing, to really enjoy the event and the endorphins that come with interacting with people, and it not being all about relieving the withdrawal. You can really meet and share and learn about other people, and let social interactions run naturally without constant interruption.

19.

Smoking Relieves Boredom

Smoking relieving boredom is another of the central truths for many smokers, but one that is even more obviously nonsensical than most of the others, and even easier to dismantle. After all, what is boredom? It's the state of not having enough to occupy your mind. We are all different—some of us are more intelligent than others, and we all take interest in different things. But whoever you are, however intelligent or otherwise you consider yourself to be, and whatever interests you, if you don't have enough to occupy your mind, you will be bored.

Smoking involves reaching for the pack, opening it, taking out a cigarette, putting it into your mouth, taking a lighter, lighting the cigarette, drawing on it and inhaling the smoke. You then need to make sure the ash ends up in an ashtray or something similar, and you then need to put out the cigarette when you've finished it.

Vaping is different, there's a lot more on the tech side to get the thing up and running, but once it's there there's even less to do. Put it in your mouth, press a button, and suck the vapor in. Job done.

Neither of these requires a massive amount of brainpower, even if you don't consider intelligence to be your strongest point. The idea that the motor tasks required to smoke or vape might be enough to keep you engaged and amused for a few hours on end is frankly ridiculous. So how on earth do we end up with this very deeply held belief that smoking can relieve boredom?

Remember when we covered socializing, how there's an extrovert/introvert scale? If you are an introvert you are comfortable being on your own; if you're an extrovert you like being with other people. It's important to remember that most people aren't one or the other but fall somewhere on the scale. Even very introverted people like or need some social interaction, even if rarely and with a very small number of people (even just one) with whom they are very comfortable and relaxed. At the other end, even very extroverted people need some time alone. The fact is that most people actually like sitting down on their own for a bit, and need to do it. It gives them a chance to quietly digest what they've experienced and what is going on in their lives. Not just the big things, but also the little day-to-day things.

When you are addicted to nicotine, you cannot sit down and enjoy the moment, and just have a few quiet moments to yourself, because the withdrawal kicks in, and then the craving. So when you sit down and you are *not* smoking, you feel bored because the time starts to weigh heavy; but this is because all you're doing is craving. We get frustrated and irritated because we feel like all we are doing is sitting and thinking about smoking. The problem is exacerbated because a non-smoker in this situation, if they had time on their hands and didn't feel like just sitting quietly for a bit, would read a book, put on the TV, play a game, message a friend, or any one of numerous other things people the world over do when they have a few moments to themselves. The trouble is that when the smoker or vaper who is denied their source of nicotine—for whatever reason; maybe they are trying to stop, or are in a situation where they can't smoke—is in that situation, they can't do any of those things very comfortably because the withdrawal is slowly building.

Although on a pain scale of 1 to 10, the withdrawal is right down at the bottom, it is hugely distracting because it sets off the craving process. As we've covered previously, the craving process has five stages and it becomes increasingly distracting and torturous as the stages progress. But even the first stage (fantasizing about what it would be like to smoke) is hugely distracting. It makes it very hard to concentrate on reading, watching TV, playing a game, messaging a friend, or the like. All of these pleasant ways to spend your time are pleasant if you "lose yourself" in the activity. What this means is that a substantial amount of your mental capability is taken up with the event, such that you forget about what else is going on around you. We covered previously how the human brain is capable of thinking of a finite number of things at any one time, but it's worth bearing in mind that something like messaging a friend, for example, doesn't count as one thing. When you are messaging a friend, there will be several things within that to occupy your mind; there may be multiple topics you are discussing, and each one of those will have subtopics, if you like, that will each count as a single thing. So while messaging a friend, you may be talking about another friend, their relationships, what you've been up to, what they are up to, and pretty soon you've got many mental balls in the air and your attention is fully taken up with your messaging. Likewise, reading a novel involves keeping in mind plots, subplots, the scene, the conversation, characters, and action, and pretty soon (if it's a good book) you'll find you're immersed in it.

But the trouble is that when you don't feel 100 percent, when you've got a bit of brain fog, losing yourself in anything is going to be harder. The actual physiological withdrawal from nicotine is already going to make losing yourself in something slightly harder. But this isn't even the real issue, the real issue is—as it always is—the craving. When 90 percent of your mind is taken up with fantasizing about something you can't have, then you have zero chance of losing yourself in any activity. In fact, forget losing yourself in it, you'll be lucky to be able to engage in it at all.

So what happens? You end up doing nothing, just feeling frustrated and confined and *bored*!

So then, what if end up smoking, vaping, or dipping? The biggest and most important thing is that the craving ends; after all, you aren't going to be sitting there fantasizing about doing something that you're already doing, and you aren't going to be agonizing over whether to do something if you're already doing it. What you do is, you free up your mind. In removing the craving you free it to then concentrate on something else, like a book or a game or the TV or messaging a friend. Whatever it is, you are no longer bored!

Can you see the same basic mechanism at work here? How nicotine takes away and then only partially restores? Imagine if you are homeless and are forced to live on the streets. When it rains you get wet, when it's cold you freeze, when it's hot you bake. You have no comfortable bed to lie on, only the filthy ground. People walk past you and ignore you, or look at you with disgust or with pity. You have nowhere to wash, either yourself or your clothes, so you are filthy and you smell.

The worst of it is that you *do* own a house. It's not an amazing house, it's not a mansion, but it's a decent, perfect house for you. In there you have a bath, a shower, a bed, central heating and air-conditioning, everything you could want in a house. It's yours and it's perfect, but you can't go in there. But why?

Because there's a devious and unscrupulous organization, Nicotine Inc., that's used trickery and forgery and every underhanded move in the book to repossess your house. There is now a thug of a doorman at the front door all the time and you are only let in for short periods at a time—after you pay an exorbitant amount of money for the privilege of getting into your own home!

As time goes by, the length of time that you're allowed in the house gets shorter and shorter. It used to be that you'd make a payment and be allowed to spend a whole week in the house. Incrementally, that time has been whittled down, and now you make a payment and you get only an hour or so in the house, and you know full well that as more years pass you're going to end up getting only a few minutes in the house for each payment. Eventually, you'll be paying constantly.

If that wasn't bad enough, Nicotine Inc. is a very bad house owner. They don't care about the house at all, after all, the house is nothing to them, all they're interested in is getting those payments from you. The house doesn't get cleaned, let alone repaired. It's already getting dirty and scruffy inside, so you are being let into a place that is less and less pleasant to visit. It's also only a matter of time before there's some serious problem, like the roof leaking, which will let the rain and weather in. After that it won't be long before the house is a ruin.

Smoking and vaping feels like it is allowing us access to something—a building that we very much want to go into. That cigarette or vape opens the door to that building and allows us to enter, and we are so very grateful. We scrape and beg and pay money and our health and self-respect to it to allow us in, but what we've forgotten is that the building is ours! We have every right to be there, and to live there all the time, not only when we are able to pay yet more to the nicotine gatekeeper who allows us back in.

That house is your life. YOURS. It's becoming less and less pleasant every day you allow nicotine to have control of it, and when that house is gone, so will you be. Can you see now the illusion that smoking and vaping creates? It feels like it allows us to access something wonderful, but that wonderful something is yours by right! It's something you have been thrown out of and then are let back in only on occasion, and every time you go back into that place, it's slightly less pleasant than it should be.

This is not to say that when you quit you won't have bad days, everyone does. But you will be better able to take the bad in stride, to deal with it without becoming totally derailed. Think of that causeway. There will be things in life that blow you clean off your feet, but these should be rare events, not daily or weekly occurrences.

Smoking doesn't relieve boredom, it just removes your ability to occupy yourself, and then partially restores it. In fact, because of the way in which smoking impacts heart rate and energy levels, it places a lot of vigorous physical activities well outside of our comfort zone. Smokers and vapers often find they give up sports and physical pastimes years before they would otherwise due to the impact of nicotine on their fitness and energy levels. People who would otherwise spend years or even decades playing sports they enjoyed find they enjoy them less and less as their fitness is prematurely eroded, and so they give them up. Even simple things like going for a walk become less and less easy and less and less enjoyable.

20.

Why Quitting Is So Hard
and Why Quitting Is So Easy

A contradiction, right? Something can't be hard *and* easy, can it? No, it can't—well, not in exactly the same circumstances, anyway. But it can be hard if we do it one way, and easy if we do it another. We humans have a great advantage over other animals: we can use our imagination and ability to communicate to run through events before they happen, to visualize them, and we can use this ability to anticipate potential pitfalls. But the main benefit from doing this is that we can actually dissect the entire process of quitting, start to understand why it's so hard, and make a plan to circumnavigate those parts that make it difficult.

So let's use a hypothetical person, Ms. X, who is in the process of smoking what she hopes will be her last ever cigarette. She's sick of smoking at the moment. Remember the two elements of ambition, being critical of what we have and idolizing what we don't have? Ms. X has been smoking for years, she's immersed in the reality of it, and it's grim. The cough, the sore throat, the heavy feeling, the cost, the smell, the feeling of being controlled by something unnatural and ominous, the long-term health concerns, and all for a "pleasure" that a significant number of people seem able to live without perfectly happily. She's sick of the whole thing and, at the moment, is all fired up to stop. She's determined and resolute. This time she will not fail! The only problem is that she has no understanding at all about smoking and nicotine addiction. She extinguishes that cigarette, throws the butt away, and throws her remaining cigarettes in the bin (remembering first to soak them in water so she can't pick them out of the bin twenty minutes later to smoke them). She's all set!

Of course as soon as she stops supplying her body with nicotine, the withdrawal kicks in. As the nicotine starts to wear off, it leaves behind it a chemical imbalance that has been caused by all the previous cigarettes she's ever smoked. It's a subtle feeling but an unpleasant one. It's a feeling of being slightly unable to focus, of feeling something's not quite right, of finding everything hard to get to grips with. There are three things we need to bear in mind about this.

First and most obviously, this feeling will build and build and cannot be avoided because it is a physiological reaction and it isn't affected by how determined or otherwise she is not to smoke.

Second, her brain will interpret this feeling as "I need a smoke." This is a feeling she's experienced many times a day for however many years she's been smoking, and her subconscious brain has learned through repetition that a smoke will relieve that feeling. Every one of those thousands, tens of thousands, or even hundreds of thousands of cigarettes she's smoked have hammered that message more and more deeply into her subconscious. So as the withdrawal starts to kick in, the thought of a smoke will enter Ms. X's mind.

Third, the withdrawal erodes her confidence, ability to cope, resolution, determination, and her desire to get to grips with difficult things. Remember when we talked previously about when an animal is healthy and at its best physically, it feels adventurous and confident? Able and willing to take on challenges, feeling like it can do anything? No, this isn't just a feeling you get when you're young, it's a feeling you should have throughout your whole life providing you aren't constantly messing with and disrupting the chemical balance in your brain. And when an animal isn't feeling well, it goes the other way, it feels timid and afraid and it just wants to hide away somewhere safe and quiet, to rest and recuperate. It's nature's way of ensuring that animals that are healthy and are at their best get out there to live life, to find food, new territory, a mate, and so on. And if an animal is injured or unwell, it doesn't go out there where it may need to fight or run, it hides away until its body has had a chance to repair itself or fight off whatever infection it has.

So as the withdrawal kicks in Ms. X becomes less confident, less resolute, more unsure of herself, more inclined to put off anything difficult until another day. And what difficult thing is she dealing with at the moment? That's right, quitting smoking!

Some attempts to quit just result in giving in to the craving. Sometimes a person may just decide they can't face life without a smoke, but a significant number of attempts to quit are abandoned because "now isn't a good time to quit." We don't abandon our attempt to quit because we decide we'd like to smoke for the rest of our lives; rather, we just decide that we've picked a bad time to stop and we'll have better luck if we try another time. Some people think this is just excuse making, that we want to smoke so we just keep putting off our quitting day. There may be an element of truth to this, but in fact there is a physiological reason, too.

The withdrawal erodes our resolve, it undermines our determination, it makes us want to put off that difficult day for as long as possible. While Ms. X was smoking that last cigarette and the nicotine was flowing into her bloodstream, she was almost as confident and resilient as she was she was before she started smoking. She was absolutely determined to quit and was mentally strong enough to give it a pretty good go. But as she cut off that supply of nicotine her confidence and ability to rise to the challenge started to go with it. Pretty soon her mindset started to switch from "today's the day" to "tomorrow's looking far better." On a subconscious level we realize that we just aren't at our best, that without this confident determined feeling anything we attempt is going to be far harder, so we are far better off postponing the attempt to quit. A very strong urge to delay kicks in.

So the three points about the withdrawal that we need to keep in mind are that, first, we cannot avoid it, second, that it creates the thought of a smoke, and third, it creates a desire to postpone quitting. Let's now look at the second of these: the thought of a smoke.

To appreciate the effect of this, we need to think back to the chapter on cravings. Remember there are five stages in the process of craving: the thought of smoking or vaping, fantasizing about it, anticipation, subconscious decision-making, and the search for excuses. What it amounts to is torturing ourselves with the thought of something; like being really hungry and fantasizing about our favorite food.

So craving is made up of five constituent stages or parts and the linked process is:

Thought of smoking—fantasizing—anticipation—subconscious decision—search for excuses

Most people do not appreciate the constituent parts of this process, they just see it as craving, so their understanding looks more like this:

Thought of smoking = craving

Many people don't even appreciate that there are two stages above; so, for most people, what the experience comes down to is this:

I think of smoking and I'm craving.

It's a one-step process as far as they are concerned, so the only way they can think of to deal with it is to not think about smoking, or to resist the craving.

For a smoker, to not think about smoking is impossible. The withdrawal is kicking in and won't start tailing off for a few days, and your brain is fully conditioned to reach for a cigarette to alleviate it. Going back to our example, the thought of smoking will be constantly popping into Ms. X's mind for the first few days, indeed it's likely that she'll be thinking of it incessantly because the withdrawal will be there incessantly. But even after the withdrawal is gone, the thought of smoking will continue to enter her mind. She is going to see people smoking, she's going to talk to people who smoke, she's going to go to shops that sell cigarettes, she's going to read books and watch TV programs and films in which people smoke, and she's going to enter situations and places, and attend events where she used to smoke. If her attempt to quit is reliant on her "not thinking about smoking," then she's already failed.

So the only thing she can do is resist the temptation. As we dealt with before, the craving becomes more intense as we go through the stages of it, and while we may not go through all the stages, we do go through them in order. So sitting there fantasizing about having a smoke is downright torturous. When you start to anticipate the actual possibility of having a smoke, you up it a level, and if the subconscious kicks in and you start the search for excuses, you're now in a panic, on the verge of giving in, and just desperately looking for any old justification to allow you to do what you've already decided to do. So Ms. X will fantasize about smoking, and it won't be pleasant. It will take up all her thoughts and while she does this she will disengage from whatever else she is supposed to be doing, be that work, time with her friends, or relaxing at home. If she's lucky, and if her determination not to smoke started off strong enough, she may never progress to the anticipation stage of craving (in fact this is what happens to most people in the early stage; their resolution is strong enough to carry them through and although they spend virtually all their time thinking about how good it would be to smoke, they may be able to avoid upping the torture to the next level).

So let's assume the best case, that Ms. X fantasizes about it, which won't be pleasant, but she manages to resist it because her resolve to quit prevents her from allowing the possibility of smoking to enter her mind, which is where the torture is concentrated.

So in this very early stage of quitting Ms. X has three hurdles to overcome: the withdrawal, the fantasizing part of craving, and a very strong feeling that she's picked a very bad time to quit, and that if she'd just picked another time she'd find it far easier. After all, when she's feeling at her best she's very determined to quit. But she's not in the best place right now; in fact, she's feeling pretty under par.

One of the main problems with this is, when will it end? Most people these days appreciate that there is a withdrawal from nicotine (even if it is not very well understood), so there will be an element of understanding on Ms. X's part that this unpleasant phase will pass, but equally *she wants a cigarette because she enjoys them* (or at least believes she enjoys them). While the smoker who is trying to quit appreciates that there is an element that involves withdrawal, they've also no doubt spoken to many people who have quit for extended periods but who still desperately want to smoke. You do come across them, people who may have quit for months or even years and who will tell you that they still desperately crave a cigarette on occasion. So while we appreciate that some of this unpleasant phase will pass, we also fear that much of it won't. A lot of the unpleasantness here is wanting something that we can't have, and if people still want to smoke after quitting for years, isn't it the case that much if not most of this unpleasantness is going to continue indefinitely?

Humans can put up with a lot as long as they know it is for a finite period. Seeing a point in the future when suffering will end is incredibly important because it allows us hope. But if there is no end to the suffering there is no hope, instead there is despair. This the crux of why smoking is so hard to quit if you go about it in the wrong way. Smoking may seem irrational both to the non-smoker and to the smoker, but when we understand it, it isn't irrational at all. Forget the physical withdrawal, even without that Ms. X is not in a good place. She's unhappy, wanting something she can't have, torturing herself with the thought of it; she's disengaged from life, she can't concentrate on work, relaxing, or seeing friends, and the worst is that she suspects (either consciously or subconsciously) that this misery will carry on for the rest of her life or until she smokes again. In fact the most rational course of action in this situation is just to smoke. Let's say Ms. X is forty and expects to live until she's eighty if she quits or sixty if she carries on smoking. So if she smokes she'll have twenty years of life left, and if she quits she'll have forty years of life left. But if you had a choice of forty years of misery and despair or twenty years of a normal, decent life, which would you choose? I know what I'd choose, and it wouldn't be forty years of misery!

But let's assume that Ms. X is one of the brave few who keeps plodding on with this. The physical withdrawal from nicotine reaches its peak around three to five days after quitting, then it starts to tail off and is entirely gone after two to four weeks. A lot of people mistakenly think that after this stage it's job done, problem solved, but, of course, that isn't the case.

Remember chapter 11, where we deconstructed the myth that smoking relieves stress? Again, every smoker has two types of stress, the stress from a genuinely stressful event, and the additional stress from the nicotine withdrawal. Smoking will only relieve the nicotine withdrawal stress, not the real stress, but neither your conscious nor your subconscious will be able to differentiate between the two; all most people understand of the situation is that smoking relieves stress. So even when the withdrawal is done, when you next encounter any stress you will want a cigarette because you retain the belief that a cigarette will help. Of course it will be of no physical help at this stage because there's no withdrawal to relieve, but your subconscious won't know this.

This is further confused by craving. Let's assume Ms. X has survived the withdrawal phase totally and is completely through it. She then encounters a bit of stress. It doesn't need to be a huge, life-changing event, it can just be one of those things that we all encounter on a day-to-day basis. But because she retains a belief that smoking does indeed relieve stress, the thought of having a smoke enters her mind. Because she doesn't really understand the processes involved, she does the natural thing, which is to start to test it out in her mind. She thinks about taking a cigarette out of the pack, the firm, crisp feel of it; she thinks about how it would feel to put it in her mouth, to light it, to draw the smoke into her lungs and to feel (so she believes) all the stress just melt away. As soon as she embarks on this thought process she's worse off because no matter how stressed she was previously, she's now craving something she can't have and is torturing herself with the thought of it. She can't concentrate and she can't focus because her attention is now exclusively concentrating on this unpleasant and ultimately frustrating internal debate.

If Ms. X smokes now, physically the cigarette won't do anything for her at all because there's no withdrawal to relieve. In fact, she's likely to be worse off because nicotine is a very strong stimulant and it isn't particularly pleasant if you aren't physically addicted to it; it tends to leave people anxious and twitched up (rather like drinking too much caffeine). But what smoking at this stage *will* do is end the craving. It will end the unpleasant internal debate and torture, so Ms. X can then turn her mind to the issue at hand. The net result is that she does genuinely feel better for having had a smoke, she's strengthened her belief that smoking does help with stress, and she's also strengthened her belief that, no matter how long you've stopped for, smoking is pleasant and a way of relieving stress.

Another key aspect here is that there are two immediate physical benefits to quitting smoking. The first is to lose that heavy, drained feeling you get from constantly artificially accelerating your heart rate. The other is to regain whatever mental resilience you had before you started smoking. The trouble with these two elements is that they are usually missed. That heavy feeling is something we experience when we smoke, and most people aren't even aware that it exists. So when we stop we don't appreciate how wonderful it is to not experience it anymore. It's also gradual: from one moment to the next we don't feel any different, so although it's a huge benefit of stopping, it's one that most people don't appreciate.

The other aspect is that as the withdrawal dissipates we go back to a level of confidence and mental resilience that we haven't experienced since we started smoking. But again, it's gradual; we return to that state over a few weeks and we don't feel very different from one day to the next. If you're not looking for it, it can be very easy to miss. So although Ms. X is almost immediately better off for stopping, and while this improvement will continue to increase over the coming days and weeks, she is likely to miss it, to not appreciate it, not least because she will be craving and so more miserable overall. Most of us are incredibly busy, we are constantly rushing from one thing to the next and feeling like there just aren't enough hours in the day. We tend to experience life as one great lump of feelings and judge it overall because we simply don't have the time and mental bandwidth to break it down into its constituent parts and analyze and consider each part of it. So although Ms. X is feeling physically better every single day that goes by, she probably doesn't feel better overall because she's spending most of her time craving, so she totally misses the very substantial and immediate physical gains and instead looks at the net result, which is that she feels worse overall. This is also why some people will tell you that they stopped vaping or smoking and felt awful for doing so. Their experience is that when they quit they felt worse, and it would never dawn on them to deconstruct it into its constituent parts and analyze each one to find the actual root cause.

So, unfortunately, Ms. X's problems don't stop when the withdrawal does. In certain key aspects, they get worse. The general conception of quitting is that you quit, it's hard, but things slowly improve. In some ways, of course, things do improve (for example the withdrawal disappears); in some ways they remain much the same (like craving) and in some ways the more time passes, the harder things get. This is where

Fading Affect Bias, ambition, and the return of our mental resilience start to work against us.

Remember the concept of Fading Affect Bias? We have a tendency to look back on past events and recall them more positively than they actually were. Remember ambition, how we tend to be critical of what we have and idolize what we don't have? Between these two we start thinking back on our smoking fondly, we start to idolize it. Forgotten are the vast majority of cigarettes that we smoked without even really being aware of them or didn't really enjoy, and instead we focus on the one or two that we really believed we enjoyed. Suddenly, the reality of life as a smoker is forgotten and we start to imagine a weird, unrealistic fantasy of what it was like, where it was all fun and pleasant and beautiful. If this wasn't damaging enough, our mental resilience and strength of character has returned. Why is this damaging? Because now that we are back to our usual, confident self, the idea of being addicted to something becomes alien. Now that we are complete and competent and capable, the thought of being forced to do something we hate seems unimaginable. We forget the mental state we were in where we needed our little drug to get us through the day; it seems incomprehensible, impossible. So the more time that passes, the more fondly we think of smoking, and the less able we are to remember what it was like to be addicted to it.

In short, our fear of becoming addicted to it again starts to erode. Coupled with this is our clear memory of how, when we first started smoking, we were able to take it or leave it, or that we only smoked on weekends or at social occasions. Logically, now that we've quit for a bit, we should be able to start again and return to that stage. After all, we've just successfully quit, right? If we can cut out all cigarettes we should be able to just smoke one or two. Quitting requires resisting cigarettes all the time, whereas if we just smoke one or two we only have to resist cigarettes most of the time—and resisting more of the time must be easier than resisting all the time, right?

When we understand the nature of addiction and craving we can see that this reasoning is fundamentally flawed; a significant part of addiction is craving, and a significant part of craving is allowing the possibility of taking the drug. In allowing the possibility of even one dose of the drug, we give full power to the addiction because suddenly smoking or vaping is back on the menu. So we know that allowing even a single puff is fatal, but most smokers don't have this knowledge, and these thoughts can be very compelling.

So, as you can see, when Ms. X quit the odds were stacked against her and these odds continued to be stacked against her for years to come. The dynamics change, and the individual physical, physiological, and psychological elements involved all change over time, but throughout that time she's facing an uphill struggle. And if she is one of the lucky few who manages to grit her teeth and make it through to the end of her life without smoking again? The chances are she will have gone through life missing smoking, regularly thinking about it and how wonderful it was, craving it, and generally feeling like she's been missing out because she quit. She'll largely take the benefits for granted or miss them, and every time she sees someone smoking she will envy them and wish she could still enjoy that wonderful smoke, just like they are. She's no doubt better off than if she was smoking, but she's had to go through a tough process, and it's never really ended for her. It's been a constant battle for her whole life, albeit a battle that may have become less fierce as time passed. This is one of the central horrors of addiction, it can pollute your entire life. You aren't happy when you're taking the drug, and you aren't happy when you stop.

So that's why quitting smoking is so hard. Let's now look at why it's so easy.

This time we are going to follow Ms. Y. Ms. Y is smart and has done her homework and a lot of preparation. Ms. Y has done a real deep dive on smoking, she understands the dynamics involved and she understands them well. Ms. Y isn't making a reluctant attempt to stop—Ms. Y can't wait to start her new life. In fact, Ms. Y is pretty angry about the whole thing. Going back to our analogy from the previous chapter, Ms. Y understands now that she's been conned for years by Nicotine Inc. They have stolen her house and she's spent years on the streets, but that ends today! Ms. Y knows she's going to have to face the physical withdrawal and she does not care. Even if the withdrawal goes on for years and is deeply painful, she's not going to back down. But she knows it won't be that bad. In fact, she knows exactly what's involved: the withdrawal will involve a bit of brain fog, some disorientation, some inability to focus. She knows those symptoms will get worse and worse and peak around three to five days, then they are going to fade away until they're totally gone in about two to four weeks.

Ms. Y has always known she was pretty unfit and tired, and a bit overweight. She's always chalked it up to getting older and to life generally. Now she realizes how much of it is related to her smoking, and she's riled up! She understands how all the benefits she thought she was getting out of smoking are false, how for everything smoking gave her it had first taken away at least twice as much. Ms. Y cannot wait to get back to that feeling of resilience, confidence, and vibrancy. She wants to get out there and enjoy life and rise to any challenges, a feeling that smoking has taken from her.

Ms. Y knows she's living on the streets at the moment and that Nicotine Inc is in possession of her precious house, her *life*. But she's learned an important secret: that the power nicotine has all comes from her. Every time she uses it, its power increases. The secret is that all she has to do is stop and its hold on her will eventually crumble into the dust.

So Ms. Y sits down and smokes her last cigarette. In fact, she doesn't even want it, but it's a symbolic gesture to her. It marks the end of her old life, and the beginning of her new one. It marks the demise of her enemy, the organization that has hurt her and damaged her for so long, that has conned her and taken advantage of her. She puts that last cigarette out with a feeling of relief and power; she knows things aren't going to be plain sailing, she hasn't got her house back yet, but she knows that whatever happens, whatever life may throw at her, she's never going to make one more payment to Nicotine Inc. and that without that money the organization cannot survive. By extinguishing her last ever cigarette she has destroyed it as surely as if she'd burned it to the ground. It's just that this death blow will take some time for its fatal effects to be felt. So much the better, she can watch its death throes with glee! It certainly doesn't deserve a quick and easy death.

So Ms. Y extinguishes her final cigarette with excitement. As soon as that final cigarette is put out, the withdrawal starts to kick in. But you know what? That's fine. Ms. Y was expecting it, she's ready to put up with it, and most important of all, she knows full well it will only last a few days. It's not so bad, it's not a pleasant feeling, but it's not really any worse than having a cold or even a touch of the flu. She's well prepared to go through this and a lot more to see that vile organization that conned her out of her lovely home ground into the dust!

Very soon, if not immediately, the thought of smoking a cigarette enters Ms. Y's mind. But again she's totally prepared for this, she's been expecting it. She knows how things work, she knows the pathetic tricks Nicotine Inc. uses to compel her to destroy herself. It's no longer a powerful and fearful organization; in fact, it's quite pathetic. Like a magician with just a few simple tricks that get repeated over and over: when you don't understand the tricks they can seem amazing—awe-inspiring, even. But when you know how they're done and that they are just simple tricks repeated over and over in different formats, the whole show loses its ability to enthrall you. In fact, it's just time to get up and walk away from it. You're bored with the whole pathetic performance. It no longer has any power over you.

So the thought of a cigarette enters Ms. Y's mind, but here's the clever part. Because she knows how things work, her thought process from this point is very different from Ms. X's. Whereas Ms. X at this point started fantasizing about how wonderful it would be to smoke and started torturing herself with the thought of it, Ms. Y does something quite different, because for Ms. Y there is no more fantasy, only cold, hard facts. When Ms. Y thinks about smoking she doesn't fantasize about it, she thinks about how that cigarette will send her heart rate through the roof, making her feel heavy and lethargic and weak, and she's thinking about how every extra beat of her heart caused by the stimulating effects of the nicotine is eroding her fitness, weakening her, and taking her one heartbeat closer to the grave. She's thinking about how the feeling of the smoke going into her lungs is like choking. It is taking a cancerous poison into her delicate, precious lungs, and she knows the only reason she ever thought it was a good feeling was because her brain was fooled by the effects of the drug. She remembers that the natural reaction is to cough and splutter to get the filth out. And most of all she's thinking how that wonderful feeling she'd get from a smoke—focus and clarity of mind, confidence and contentment—is all from relieving an unpleasant feeling caused by all the previous doses of nicotine, and how, in a few days, she's going to have that wonderful feeling all the time, all day, every day, and she won't have to poison herself to get it ever again. She's going to get her house back!

So Ms. Y does not fantasize; instead, her thoughts are firmly based in reality, and she certainly does not entertain the possibility of actually having a smoke—in fact, that possibility has never been further from her mind. That is the one absolute for her, there's no way she's going back, no way she's going to start giving power back to Nicotine Inc. and that insidious doorman. In short, Ms. Y does not crave. This is the key. Knowledge and understanding have led to certainty, and both of these together mean no craving. Is Ms. Y 100 percent sure she won't slip into the old thought processes, that she will never, ever start fantasizing about a smoke? Of course not—the thought of smoking is going to be entering her mind almost incessantly for those first few days, and at odd times she may start fantasizing before she has a chance to catch herself. But she's totally relaxed about that. When it happens she's going to calmly remind herself about the reality and put herself back on track.

She also knows that she's going to feel a bit odd for those first few days for another reason: she'll have less to do. Smoking is a physical act, and there are small but important actions involved in being a smoker that very quickly become incorporated into your daily routine if you smoke. Leaving the house? Quick checklist: keys, phone, wallet or purse, cigarettes, and lighter (or vape). These last two are no longer required. Sitting down after getting home from work and lighting a cigarette? No longer required. There will be a general feeling that something is missing, and there is: a significant number of physical actions will no longer be required, it can almost feel like you've just grown an extra couple of arms and you feel like you need to do something with them but you aren't sure what! This is a purely motor reaction and will usually settle down even before the physical withdrawal has disappeared.

Ms. Y is taking this one step further: when the thought of a smoke enters her mind she's not just going to stick with reality to stop the fantasy of craving, she's going to remind herself how happy she is to be free. Every time the thought of a cigarette enters her head and she doesn't smoke, she envisions denying a payment to Nicotine Inc. The thoughts are a payment demand from Nicotine Inc. and she knows they are going to send some really bullying and threatening letters. But Ms. Y knows that it's totally within her power to refuse to make that payment, and every time she refuses, the organization dies a little more.

So Ms. Y has the thought of a smoke hitting her constantly, but she never lets a craving take hold because she reins in her thoughts before she starts fantasizing, and she certainly never doubts her decision to quit or allows herself to consider the possibility of taking a smoke. She may not feel too good physically, she may feel woolly-headed, she may have brain fog, she may feel lethargic, restless, out of sorts, headachy, she may sleep more, she may sleep less, but she sees every last one of these physical manifestations for exactly what they are: the death throes of her addiction. She knows that within a few days, maybe a few weeks at the outside, all of these will be gone. She knows that all of these things have been caused by her smoking and soon they will be gone, never to return.

So the days slip by for Ms. Y, perhaps not the best days of her life physically, but mentally she already feels better than she has in years because she's finally winning a battle she thought she could never win. At last those dark shadows at the back of her mind, that cognitive dissonance, is gone. She doesn't have to wait until the withdrawal has gone to enjoy that; she may have felt those dark clouds lifting before she even smoked her last cigarette. And as the days turn into weeks the physical withdrawal disappears and Ms. Y starts to feel physically better than she has in years. She feels more confident, stronger, more energetic, and happier. She knows she's going to have bad days, but she also knows that now she is better able to deal with those bad days. This return to physical and mental strength isn't lost on Ms. Y, it's a subtle change and easy to miss for many, but she's specifically looking out for it and so she notices. Pretty soon she feels better than she ever did when she was smoking, she feels better all the time, even better than she did when having that all-important first smoke of the day.

As the weeks turn into months, Ms. Y starts to forget how it felt to be in the control of nicotine, how she could ever have ended up weak and scared enough to have been in its thrall. She also finds that she thinks quite fondly of smoking when she looks back on her smoking years, but again, this is all fine. She knows about Fading Affect Bias, about ambition, she understands the tendency to glorify what we don't have, so she knows these thoughts are false. When she gets these thoughts, she sees them for what they are: distortions caused by the lens of time. She remembers the reality of her life as a smoker, the heavy feeling, the lack of energy, the worry about her health, the cost—everything that made her so desperately keen to quit in the first place. She's on guard for these thoughts, but other than this she just gets on with her new and vastly improved life.

The stories of Ms. X and Ms. Y illustrate the physical, chemical, physiological, and psychological processes at play when we try to quit and show how different the experience is when you arm yourself with knowledge, do some preparation, and change your mindset. Quitting is easy when we truly change our core beliefs about smoking and vaping. We do this by educating ourselves about what smoking and vaping really are, what nicotine actually does, and, crucially, what it does not do for us.

21.

Self-Image

Self-image is a huge, often overlooked, part of our lives. It's far more than just what we wear and how we think we look on any particular day. It goes to very core of who we are. Our ethnicity, political views, gender identity, the place where we live, our job, level of education, hobbies, family history, favorite foods, and more all make up who we are and how we perceive ourselves.

These defining qualities and characteristics shape who we are and how we see ourselves, and we act in accordance with this image. In other words, it both creates and reinforces who we are. For example, if you see yourself as someone who is quiet and sensible, you are going to react to a situation very differently than someone who considers themselves to be physical, reactive, and forthright. Imagine someone who considers themselves to be intelligent, sensible, and intellectual. They accidentally cut someone off on the freeway. At the next set of lights they get caught on red and that person they cut off pulls over next to them and starts shouting at them. They aren't going to get sucked into a demeaning, vulgar, and ultimately pointless public shouting match. They just sit there and stare pointedly ahead, wait for the lights to change, and eventually drive off, grateful that they are not like the Neanderthal who just pulled up next to them.

But what if exactly the same thing happened to someone who's just finished military basic training? Someone who has spent the last few months being taught to be aggressive, to stand firm, to never give an inch. Someone who has had their confidence in their physical ability to fight and win built up, someone who has been trained to meet aggression with an even more overwhelming aggression, someone who has been taught that it's better to fight and lose than to back down? How do you think this person might react to a road rage incident?

Part of our self-image is a tendency to look down a bit on people who aren't us. If you see yourself as clever and well educated, but maybe not very physical, you may look down on people who are "all brawn and no brains." Equally, if you think your strength lies in your physical side and not your education, you may be inclined to sneer a bit at those who rely on so-called book smarts and have no physical ability. This is a kind of self-protection and it's a simple facet of human existence.

When you smoke or vape it affects who you are and what you do. It affects your ability to exercise, and you tend to spend your time doing things that allow you to smoke or vape freely and also to focus on things that don't involve too much physical activity. It's not just the smoking or vaping that becomes a part of who we are, but it limits and dictates the activities we take part in, and so that becomes a part of our self-image. We then start to look down a bit at anyone who is different than us.

Smokers and vapers tend to look down a bit on people who don't smoke or vape.

We start to see them as fussy and persnickety, as though they are people who are obsessed with their health at the expense of their quality of life. This illusion is exacerbated by the effect smoking has on our heart rate. Because smoking increases our heart rate so dramatically, exercise is very difficult and intensely uncomfortable, even painful, for us. As a result, we just sort of assume that everyone finds exercise that unpleasant. Our experiences (in this case, that physical exercise is intensely difficult) become our reality, and our natural tendency is to assume that this is reality for everyone. So, when we meet people who get up and go for a five-mile run every morning we imagine that it must be intensely painful for them, and that to undergo that level of pain they must be utterly obsessed with the length of their life or some kind of weirdo to go through that agony every day. In short, their behavior is totally incomprehensible to us and we are completely unable to relate to them.

Our tendency is to see the fault with them and not ourselves; it simply never dawns on most smokers or vapers that movement and exercise are enjoyable and pleasant for human beings, that those things release endorphins that make people feel genuinely good all day long. When you are fit and healthy, then running, walking, cycling, and other movement isn't hard work or unpleasant, it's hugely enjoyable. It feels great to get out into the world and get some ground under your feet. When we are smoking or vaping, we don't make the connection that the reason we no longer experience these positive feelings is because of the drug that we are forced to keep taking, day after day after day until it eventually kills us. Nicotine Inc. doesn't just take possession of your house and only lets you back in when you pay, it actually closes off parts of your house so you never get to enjoy it at all, not until you take back control.

Our self-image starts to be formed by our addiction and so we seek out and prefer other smokers and vapers and start to prefer their company. And we love to see famous celebrities smoking and vaping. Have you ever wondered why?

To explore this idea, it helps to first go back to how we see non-smokers—fussy, too "caught up" in life, unable to just sit back and enjoy the moment. Think about how you see yourself as a smoker or a vaper. Do you see it as a rebellious act in a society that is always vilifying smokers and vapers? Do you see it as glamorous, independent, maverick? Do you think it defines you as a risk taker? A leader? As single-minded and independent? Think now about all these qualities that you associate with your smoking.

Do you think non-smokers see you the way you see yourself? Do you think they see you as glamorous and independent, a maverick? Of course not—they see you as a nicotine addict. They feel sorry for you because you are forced to put your health in jeopardy because you're weaker than your addiction. Just as you see the daily runner as a freak, they also don't understand you. They don't think you're glamorous or rebellious, they find your behavior incomprehensible and even pathetic. They see you as physically unfit, weak, and under the power of something deeply unpleasant, and maybe even as a financial supporter of one of the most destructive industries on the entire planet.

Try to forget your self-image for the moment and see things as they really are. Which of these very different images of the smoker or vaper is correct? It can be extremely hard to get past the distorting lens of our self-image, but is it essential that we do so. Stick with the central, unarguable facts. Smoking and vaping is all about addiction to nicotine. It increases your heart rate, erodes your fitness, and leaves you feeling heavy and exhausted. Is smoking and vaping glamorous and cool? Or is it pathetic and damaging?

With any objective analysis it's clear that smoking and vaping isn't cool or sophisticated. It's simple drug addiction. But because we're compelled to keep doing it, we desperately look for ways to make it appear more palatable. One of the best ways to do this is through our smoking and vaping icons. When we see famous people smoking and vaping it puts a veneer of sophistication over the whole thing. We look at them and we see ourselves in their image. Just as when we aren't smoking we idolize it, we think of all the supposed good and none of the bad, so we do the same when we see a picture of Tom Hardy or Katy Perry vaping. When we see them, we don't think of the sore throat, the heavy feeling, the obsessing when we can't smoke. Do you think that these famous figures don't suffer the same doubts and insecurities that you do with your smoking and vaping? Do you think that their heart rate doesn't accelerate when the nicotine hits their bloodstream? That they don't feel insecure and out of sorts as the nicotine wears off?

Of course, it's not just famous people who help distort the ugly reality of our addiction, but also friends, acquaintances, and social media images. Seeing a post of a friend smoking or vaping helps us to maintain the false, glorified image we have of how *we* look smoking and vaping. We even do it ourselves. We like to see pictures of ourselves with a smoke or a vape, exhaling a huge cloud; it makes our addiction seem rebellious and mysterious. There is a psychological concept called the looking-glass self, which refers to the idea that how we see ourselves doesn't relate to who we really are, but rather to how we think others see us. Posting images of ourselves allows us to project an image of our addiction that we find most acceptable; it allows us to coat it with a veneer of acceptability.

The goal of this book is to uncover the reality of smoking, to pull out all your beliefs from your subconscious in the same way that you'd clear out a house that's filled with junk, cluttering up your living space, affecting how you feel and how you live. Only you seem to have accumulated all the stuff without making any kind of conscious decision. Did you make a conscious decision to smoke or vape all day, every day without being able to stop? Did you at any point decide that you wanted this substance to dominate your life, to control you? Did you ever make a decision that you wanted to never be able to enjoy life again unless you were inhaling this poison? Or did you just try one puff and suddenly find, weeks, months, or years down the line, that it had somehow become a crucial part of your life, a part that you simply now could not do without?

In the same way, people don't make the conscious decision to live in a cluttered house; they just seem to accumulate things and before long their entire living space is dominated by what they own. In this book, we want to help you pull that stuff out, shine the light of reason on it, and then decide if it is actually true and helping you, or if it is false and damaging, in which case you can discard it. Your addiction is your prison, and it is made up of your beliefs about smoking, the core one being the belief that life's better with a smoke. If you can get rid of these beliefs, then you can dismantle your prison, brick by brick. Your self-image as a smoker or vaper is another of these beliefs that need to be examined and reevaluated.

Coming to an objective view on many of the negative effects of smoking is fairly straightforward. For example, the dynamics of the chemical and physiological process of withdrawal, and relieving the withdrawal, is not open to individual interpretation or debate. Smoking as it relates to self-image is less clear-cut, however, for the simple reason that it is all about perception, our self-perception and the perception of others. For this reason, coming to a purely objective position is it not possible. But what we can do is try to see it in a far more realistic light.

Think now about how you perceive your smoking or vaping. Do you see it as sociable? Rebellious? Fearless? Do you think it defines you as a certain type of person? If so, what does it say about you? Maybe you think it makes you seem audacious? Or that it marks you as a member of a certain subculture that raises you above the herd?

We all have different associations with our smoking and vaping, and different ways we think it defines us. Spend some time really trying to identify the image of your "smoking self." Ask yourself, is it a realistic image?

Have you ever been out and seen someone who is dressed in a very trendy or outlandish way, but you think he or she just looks absurd? While you may think this person doesn't look as cool as they think they do, do you think they see themselves in the same way? Or do you think they think they look great? As is often the case, we can see things a lot more clearly by looking at an example with children. Think of a seven-year-old who is dressed up as Spider-Man. In his mind, that child *is* Spider-Man—clever, audacious, cool, funny, powerful. To everyone else, he's a seven-year-old playing dress-up. Which is the more realistic view? Consider this scenario and how it relates to how you perceive your smoking or vaping. You need to analyze these perceptions and see if they are realistic, if other people see you in the same way. Are you really a superhero, or just a child in a cheap polyester outfit?

Let's run through some simple, unarguable facts about smoking and vaping to help clarify our perception of it:

1. It is addiction, plain and simple. The fact that we believe we enjoy it, that we believe we still retain choice over it, does not diminish this truth. Nicotine is a drug that leaves an unpleasant feeling when it wears off and the pleasure of smoking and vaping is to take another dose of nicotine to relieve that withdrawal. This is the very definition of addiction.

2. Because nicotine increases our heart rate, it erodes our fitness and makes exercise more difficult, even hard work. There are people who are (or who will tell you at least that they are) fit and who smoke or vape, but the fact is that they are not as fit as they would be if they didn't smoke or vape. It simply isn't physiologically possible for them to be as fit as they would be if they cut out the nicotine. And their fitness levels will continue to decrease for every dose of nicotine that they take.

3. The impact nicotine has on our ability to move also affects our muscle mass. Put simply, the less you move, the more your muscles waste away.

4. Because of its effect on our appetite, smoking tends to encourage poor eating habits. This, coupled with its effect on our fitness, means smokers have a marked tendency to be overweight. Again, this is not true of everyone, but start looking at other smokers more objectively. Do they tend to be overweight, or slim? And if they are slim, do they tend to be slim and muscular, or slim and scrawny?

5. Smoking erodes our confidence and our ability to deal with the minor stresses and strains of life, and we cling to it for protection and solace. While we like to think of our behavior as something that shows us as independent and unique, it may very well be more accurate to see it as a smelly little comfort blanket, or a pacifier.

Start looking at your vaping or smoking through the eyes of someone who doesn't smoke or vape. Start seeing it as the adult pacifier that it is. It's isn't cool or rebellious; it's drug addiction, something that weakens you considerably, both physically and mentally, something that requires you to pay a large amount of money to a considerably unpleasant industry, one that makes its massive profits from destroying human health. That industry will tell you that they are simply offering a legal product for sale, and that it's the individual's choice whether to take that product or not. But addiction is the very antithesis of choice, and a person can only make a free choice when they have all the information they need. If the consumer has false information, then they are going to make the wrong decision.

Open your mind about non-smokers. What if they are not killjoys who don't want to relax or have fun—what if they are strong and in control of their lives? You may not think of yourself as strong or confident, but you will be a lot stronger and more confident when you quit nicotine than you ever were when you were addicted to it! Instead of thinking of yourself as a smoker, think of yourself as a non-smoker who is free from addiction.

ENGAGEMENT POINT

Start reevaluating your self-image. Think of the reality of being a smoker or vaper compared to the reality of being free of the confines of a drug.

22.

Is Vaping Safe?

There is a pervading myth that the human race only realized that smoking was addictive and bad for you in the 1950s, and that before that, people just smoked away happily. The 1950s may have been when the medical profession actively started to prove the link between smoking and cancer, but people have always known that smoking was bad for their health. How did they know? Because when our bodies don't feel right, we instinctively know that the substance we are putting in it isn't doing us any favors. The following is from the book *My Lady Nicotine: A Study in Smoke*, by J. M. Barrie (the author of *Peter Pan*) and was published in 1890:

> *I am much better without tobacco, and already have a difficulty in sympathizing with the man I used to be. Even to call him up, as it were, and regard him without prejudice is a difficult task, for we forget the old selves on whom we have turned our backs, as we forget a street that has been reconstructed. . . . There were nights when I awoke with a pain at my heart that made me hold my*

breath, I did not dare move. After perhaps ten minutes of dread, I
would shift my position an inch at a time. Less frequently I felt this
sting in the daytime, and believed I was dying while my friends
were talking to me.

This is the first point I would like you to consider in this chapter. Being addicted to something is, in many ways, like being in an abusive relationship, not least because there is a marked tendency in the early stages to defend and justify the abuser. When the addict takes a drug, they will always be very happy to tell you how it really does help them, how the drug is badly slandered and misunderstood, how the pressure to discourage use of the drug is financial and/or political, or even that there is a terrible conspiracy to keep this wonderful drug from benefiting the population as a whole. As the abuse continues and gets worse, as the addict is dragged down more and more, this position becomes increasingly difficult to maintain. Eventually the addict has to accept the truth: that the drug is vile and they wished they'd never started taking it in the first place. What I would ask you to do here, whether you are in that early stage of glorifying and defending your drug, or whether you have realized that it is indeed taking far more than it ever gave, is to try to undertake a frank and honest appraisal. Stop relying on this or that medical study, or what this or that organization says about smoking or vaping and whether they say it is good for you. Whoever or whatever they are, it is you who knows the most about what it is doing to your health, and it is you who will have to suffer the consequences if it is ruining your life or killing you.

Your body and brain instinctively know when something is not right. Start taking responsibility for this decision yourself. Start applying your own experience.

Although this chapter is about the health effects of vaping, to get a full understanding of it it is useful to first delve a bit more into the history of smoking, and specifically its adverse health impact. While people have always instinctively known that smoking was not good for them, the link between smoking and lung cancer first came about in the 1950s, with scientific evidence mounting in the 1980s. When the link was proven, a lot of people predicted it would mean the end of smoking, but of course that didn't happen—not even close. The reasons for this, and the tobacco industry's response, are very interesting as they provide further insight into vaping and smoking generally, and also into the perception of and response to the negative health consequences.

When research began linking smoking with lung cancer, the tobacco industry responded in an extremely clever way. We like to think that scientific studies are pretty bulletproof, but of course they aren't. Every study out there is open to criticism. Is the data accurate? Are the conclusions correct? Are there other factors that haven't been taken into account that could affect the results? That kind of thing. For example, say there's a study that tracks 2,000 people, half smoke and half don't. The half who smoke die young from various types of cancer, coronary heart disease, heart attacks, strokes, peripheral vascular disease, cerebrovascular disease, emphysema, pneumonia, and so on. The half who don't smoke don't die young from these diseases. But then people who review the study point out that the cohort who smoked lived closer to some electricity pylons, so maybe it was that that caused their health issues? Or they were also overweight, so maybe that's to blame? You get the idea—there are always ways to poke holes in even the most well-conducted research.

When studies showing the link between smoking and negative health effects were published, the tobacco industry didn't seek to refute them—it didn't even seek to deny them. All it did was to essentially say, "But what about this other factor?" and point to the one study that could suggest that the data or the conclusions of another study might not be so clear-cut.

Just to be clear: there's a lot of very reliable science showing that smoking causes serious health problems. This fact is not really in doubt anymore. There are *no* studies that show that smoking is safe. But it only takes the suggestion of doubt to sow confusion, which was the tobacco industry's strategy. It did not try to deny the links, or emphatically state that smoking wasn't bad for you but instead just pointed to one possible flaw in the existing studies, then sat back and said nothing further. What this strategy did was to sow the tiniest amount of doubt in the otherwise overwhelming data.

The tobacco industry may have chosen this strategy because it was the only thing it could do. It couldn't really try to deny the health risks because the mounting evidence was overwhelming. Equally, it couldn't just refuse to comment. Looking back, what it did was probably the only viable option, but still, it would be fascinating to know if the industry knew enough about the psychology of addiction at the time to appreciate why that move was so clever. The reason this strategy worked so well is that addicts are between a rock and a hard place. If the rock is the misery of being addicted, including all the health implications, then the hard place is the inability to quit or the fear of quitting and having to face life without their drug. On the one hand, they have the fear of dying from a smoking-related illness, on the other hand they have the fear of trying to quit.

Mostly they believe that quitting isn't an option, that life will never be quite the same without their daily little boost, so they ignore that aspect and look at the other side, the health risks. Because quitting is a no-go for them, they turn all their attention to the health risks, they look for any ray of light, no matter how small, to give them an excuse to justify their continued smoking. They will grasp at any straw to allow them to justify their continuing to smoke, and that's what the tobacco industry gave them, a mere straw. It was flimsy, pathetic, and didn't stand up to even the most cursory of examinations, but it was enough. Like the abused partner in the abusive relationship who feels like he or she cannot leave, addicts spend their mental energy seeking any excuse to keep taking their drug.

This tactic by the tobacco industry worked so well because people often read headlines without delving into the detail of an article, weighing up the pros and cons, and coming to their own view. A headline that read "Link Between Smoking and Cancer Unclear" was enough to keep a lot of people puffing away, even though if one had read the actual research, there is no doubt about the science at all. That modicum of doubt was enough; it's what the smokers were desperately searching for—an excuse to carry on! Smokers are addicted, they believe they cannot stop, so their choice is either acknowledge the health risks and continue to smoke and be very miserable and scared, or do their best to ignore the health risks and continue to smoke and be slightly less scared.

The reason why most people didn't try to understand the research more deeply is that in their heart of hearts, they knew already that smoking was bad for them. Smokers' lungs often feel tight, their heart feels like it's about to burst out of their chest whenever they stand up, and they feel heavy and lethargic and weak, so they avoid the science because they know the truth, and they cling to any flimsy straw in order to lessen the fear.

So here are the two points I would like you to have firmly in your mind: first, that you are the person who knows if vaping (or smoking) is good or bad for you, because your body tells you. Our bodies speak to us with quite a loud voice, but we've become very good at tuning it out. If you are doing something that gives you a sore throat, a cough, a dry mouth, headaches, nausea, tiredness, a dizzy or light-headed feeling when you stand up, and is making your heart race, you know it isn't doing you any favors.

The second point is that there is a marked tendency to seek to white-wash our drugs, and it is a tendency that the tobacco and vaping industries put to very good use.

With these two concepts firmly in mind, let's now take a look at whether vaping is safe. The idea behind vaping being safer than smoking is that tobacco smoke is a complex mixture of over seven thousand toxic chemicals, of which ninety-eight are associated with an increased risk of cardiovascular disease and sixty-nine of which are known to be carcino-genic. So in essence, tobacco smoke has a lot of very dangerous sub-stances in it. It also has nicotine, which is where the perceived pleasure of smoking comes in. So if you can consume only the nicotine, and cut out all the other chemicals, you can have the pleasure with less or no health risk. So does it work?

We know smoking is bad for us, but is vaping? In other words, are the nicotine and other chemicals in vapes bad for us?

The problem is that from a scientific perspective at least, the jury is out. Vaping hasn't been around long enough for us to have any clear idea of its long-term health effects. There have been deaths from vaping, but not many; on the other hand, there have been respectable organizations advising that vaping is no worse than a cup of coffee.

The problem is that we like to think that scientists are totally impar-tial, weighing only the available data and assessing it totally objectively. But the fact is that they are human—and most of them very decent humans—who desperately want to help people, and so they become pas-sionate about their point of view. There are now two very clear camps of scientists with differing opinions on vaping: those who say that even though vaping is less harmful than smoking it is still harmful and ought not to be encouraged, and those who say it is far less harmful than smok-ing, and that if we can encourage existing smokers to move to vaping, the positive health impact will be immense. So, in this view, vaping should be allowed and promoted.

The interesting thing to note here is that the two views aren't contradictory in that both camps want a healthier population, they just emphasize different, in fact mutually exclusive, ways to move toward that goal of a healthier population. We simply don't know which approach is best because the data isn't yet available. It is also I think very worthy of note that neither side claims that vaping is good for you, or has no negative health implications. They just don't agree on how damaging it is. They also don't agree on whether it is overall less damaging to promote vaping and encourage existing smokers to transition to it (even if that means some people will start vaping who otherwise may never have smoked), or whether they should discourage vaping, which would mean more people stick with smoking (which currently seems to be far more harmful), but fewer people overall become addicted to nicotine. There are a significant number of vapers out there who are quite clear that they would never smoke tobacco. Their addiction to nicotine exists purely because vaping exists. It's impossible to know which is the correct course, hence the disagreement. And in the meantime, the headlines saying that vaping is no more harmful than drinking coffee are swallowed up greedily by vapers who can use it to justify their continued intake.

Fortunately for us, even though the question of whether vaping ought to be encouraged or discouraged cannot be answered definitively at this stage, the question "Is vaping safe?" can be. It is not, because there is one irrefutable fact about nicotine that cannot be denied: it increases our heart rate without any associated increase in physical activity, and anything that does this has the long-term effect of decreasing our fitness and damaging our cardiovascular health and making heart attacks more likely. And it has the short-term effect of making us feel heavy and lethargic.

So vaping is not safe. Nicotine is a poison, and it is not safe to take it. But vaping may well be safer than smoking, and if it is—and this is the million-dollar question—is it safe enough that the benefits outweigh the health risks?

This really is the crux of the book: that there are no benefits at all to nicotine addiction. Smoking and vaping give nothing, they just take and then partially restore. Even on the most basic of physiological levels we never get more than we give. The brain very quickly acclimates to the effect of the drug so that when it wears off we feel out of sorts, so we take another dose to feel normal. So even on that very basic level we gain nothing, we just lose, then win back a little of what we've lost. When you factor in the other physiological effects, such as increased heart rate and nicotine's making us feel tired and lethargic all the time, and the psychological issue of craving, which is entirely negative, you can see that whether you are smoking, vaping, chewing, or dipping, it's all negative. The benefits are all false.

ENGAGEMENT POINT

Smokers and vapers alike spend years "protecting" their drugs, whitewashing them and clinging to any straw that justifies them continuing to take those doses of nicotine. Start letting go of those excuses now, start accepting the simple unarguable facts about nicotine and how it affects us in the short and long term.

23.

Living a Naked Life in Our Society

The reason why so many people find it hard to stop smoking or vaping is because of their core beliefs about smoking, specifically that it is enjoyable and that it helps them to cope with and enjoy life. Fortunately, these beliefs are false; they are based on misunderstandings and a misinterpretation of what consuming nicotine actually does for us. Drugs take away and then partially restore, but because the restoring process happens when we take the drug, we are fooled into thinking that the drug is actually helping us. It becomes very hard for us to see that the benefits are false because they feel so real. We feel better when we smoke, more confident, better able to deal with life, to engage in and enjoy life, so it is very hard for us to see smoking and vaping as it really is. Think about the following three points:

1. Addicts defend their drugs of choice.
2. Because relieving the withdrawal is enjoyable, we believe we enjoy smoking and so we think we are smoking through choice instead

of through compulsion: remember, there is no clear line between addiction and enjoyment.

3. Most people, when they are pushed, push back.

Given these three points, for most of the time, any addict is wasting their energy on a false battle. Drug addiction is quite rightly vilified in society. But all this means is that most of the time the addict draws up the battle lines with themselves and their drug on the one hand, and society on the other. The addict spends their time justifying what they do, fighting back against any attempt to prevent them from taking their drug (hence the pro-vaping rallies that take place). This is where their energies are concentrated as opposed to where the real battle ought to be taking place: between them and the drug that is controlling and destroying them.

Again, it is exactly the same dynamic as an abusive relationship. In the early stages, the abused person sides with the abuser against anyone who tries to interfere. This is why there is a very widespread belief that there is no point approaching an addict to offer help in quitting until they are ready to quit. If you do try to get such a person to quit, you're likely to be on the receiving end of some very choice words. The fact is that while the addict is still siding with their drug, they are simply not interested in stopping and any attempt to help them is taken as an attack, because any perceived attack on their drug is taken as an attack on their allies, their friends.

Over time, the real dynamic becomes impossible to ignore and the real battleground starts to be defined. This may give someone a desire to stop, but it doesn't make quitting any easier. Addiction is a delicate interplay between the physical and psychological processes that work together to ensure that the odds are always heavily stacked in favor of continuing to take the drug. A lot of people find that exorcising the addiction is about understanding it, and the deeper this understanding, the more thorough the exorcism.

Successfully quitting smoking isn't about putting out a cigarette, then gritting your teeth and willing yourself to do without this great pleasure. It's about not wanting to smoke anymore. It's about seeing it for what it is, stripped of all the hype and nonsense that we've built up around it to justify what we've been compelled to keep doing. It is about changing our perception; our perception of smoking or vaping, but also our perception of *not* smoking or vaping. People who don't smoke are not fussy or peculiar, they've made a simple lifestyle choice based purely on what provides the best quality of life, for the here and now as well as the future.

The general perception among smokers on quitting is that it's about sacrificing quality of life in return for length of life. Which is why so many people continue to smoke: they chose quality over quantity, which is in fact a totally understandable and sensible decision. But when you understand all the factors at play you start to understand that this perception is false; smoking takes away both quality and length. Even while you are smoking that cigarette you feel heavy and physically exhausted, and the only pleasure, the mental stimulation, amounts to feeling slightly closer to how you'd feel had you never smoked.

But the fact is that even then, even ignoring the physical drag, you don't feel as good as if you'd never smoked because there are other elements dragging you down, like those dark shadows of cognitive dissonance in the back of your mind. Some people will tell you that the best feeling in the world isn't a chemical, but I disagree. The best feelings in the world are chemicals; they are those naturally occurring chemicals such as endorphins that your brain releases that make you feel truly good. You get these when you feel mentally and physically at the top of your game. The drag effect of smoking robs you of this, so even when you are smoking you are still way behind where you could be if you quit. Quitting smoking isn't about sacrificing an immediate pleasure, it's about walking away from a total wreck.

24.

The Secret to Quitting Smoking Happily and Easily

ENGAGEMENT POINT

Look at the list of benefits you made at the end of chapter 1. These were your reasons for smoking. Look again at that list now. Go through it carefully and thoroughly. Can you see now how every last one of those is based on a false belief?

So how do we quit our nicotine addiction, easily and happily? The first step of course is preparation, which is what the rest of the book is about. But if you've jumped to this chapter to get a quick fix, then I'm afraid you've short-circuited the whole process. The reason quitting nicotine is difficult is because of our deeply held beliefs about it—it's enjoyable, it helps me relax, it helps me deal with stress, life just isn't the same without it, it helps me concentrate, it's so hard to quit, it's not really doing me any harm, the health issues are exaggerated, and so on and so forth. While you retain these beliefs, quitting will be difficult. The previous chapters are about ridding ourselves of these false beliefs. If you haven't engaged with the rest of the book to make this mental shift, then the tools in this chapter won't be useful to you.

First, a word on mindset. This book is designed to explode the myths about nicotine that keep us coming back, time and again, and we've also touched on how certainty can negate cravings. What a lot of people often find is that, as they're reading, their confidence starts to build, the certainty starts to kick in, but then they suddenly have a mini panic. It's a catch-22: you know and understand how certainty can stop cravings, but as soon as you start to doubt, you think, "But now I have uncertainty, so I'll crave" and suddenly the whole thing can start to collapse.

What you need to bear in mind is that we learn in two ways: intellectually and practically.

Learning intellectually is your book smarts. It's about (in this case) reading a book; thinking about its ideas and concepts; applying it to your smoking, vaping, or dipping; then reassessing all the information (both conscious and subconscious) that you have acquired over the years, the accumulated effect of which is to keep you coming back for more and more doses.

The practical learning comes about from getting your hands dirty with some real-life experience. Yours will come from quitting nicotine and assessing whether what you've learned in this book is correct. Do you feel better after quitting nicotine? Has your life improved, or not?

So don't worry if you find yourself swinging from confidence and euphoria to panic and doubt. Don't let it derail you. However strong you feel now, you will grow stronger as you add to your learning through practical application. This doesn't mean you won't ever have passing doubts and even possibly cravings, but as you get through them you'll learn that they aren't the massive problem you thought they were, and of course the less you worry about them, the less they happen and the less they affect you.

So the first instruction is mindset: keep positive. But there's a caveat—understand that your mindset will be affected by the withdrawal. Think of the causeway. Your causeway is about to get narrow for a few days and when the winds of misfortune blow (which they do every day, particularly for minor things like spilling your coffee or losing your keys) you can end up with your face in the dirt. In practical terms, this may mean at one moment you are feeling positive and happy and free and the next moment you're overwhelmed and on edge. This may not happen to you, but it may. You need to accept that it could happen, and if it does, then recognize it for what it is: the withdrawal. It's doing what it always did, exaggerating the stresses and strains of everyday life. Don't let it derail you. It will soon be gone, never to return.

Imagine if you go to the doctor one day with a bit of back pain. The doctor has some good news and some bad news. The bad news is that you have cancer. The good news is that you've got two options to deal with it, one very good, one not so good. The first option is to have an operation to have the cancer removed. The doctor guarantees that after the operation you'll need a week or so to recover, then you'll be absolutely fine; in fact, you'll be better than you've been for years since the cancer started. But, he also emphasizes that the operation is quite a major one, so your recovery during those few days will be a little unpleaseant. You'll be a bit groggy, maybe have a bit of pain, you certainly won't be at your best. But, after this period you'll be totally cancer-free. And what's more, the tired, drained, and weak feeling you've felt for the last few years will also subside. You may have thought you weren't feeling well because you're getting older or you are out of shape, but it turns out that it was the cancer slowly eating away at you that has been causing these symptoms. When the cancer is removed, and after the recovery, you'll feel better than you have in years, decades even.

So this is option 1. An operation, a few days feeling unwell while you recover, then total cure and a better life than you've had in years. So what's option 2? It's a packet of aspirin. The doctors tell you it will take the edge off the pain. A little bit anyway. The prognosis? The pain will keep coming back, you'll feel worse and worse as the cancer progresses, and you'll need to take more and more aspirin (and they will become increasingly less effective). You'll become increasingly weak and unable to cope, and eventually the cancer will kill you. How long will that take? It's uncertain. You could last a day, a week, a month, a year, or a decade. But this type of cancer will usually knock a good couple of decades off your life span. At least.

So this is option 2. Keep the cancer, obtain some partial relief from the pain as the cancer progresses until it eventually kills you while destroying your quality of life in the meantime. But, you'll avoid a week or two of discomfort as you recover from the operation.

You can probably see where we are going with this example. Which of these two options would you choose if you were facing a cancer diagnosis? It is not far-fetched to argue that this is the choice that confronts you now as you weigh giving up nicotine.

Let's talk now about timing. When is a good time to quit? You might be thinking you'd like to put it off. Maybe you have a birthday, or Thanksgiving or a vacation coming up, or something difficult is looming at work. But, let's consider our criteria for success. What we are trying to achieve here is to live our life, all of it, the good and the bad, without smoking or vaping. To achieve this, we have retrained our brains, but we also need to add some practical experience to this intellectual understanding. To gain this practical experience, we must get out there and live life without a smoke. We can enjoy our lives even more, now that we have the additional energy and mental resilience. When you experience this, it will strengthen your resolve.

Let's say there are certain situations that feel difficult for you to go through without smoking. These are going to be different for every individual, but they are usually things like a holiday, a night out with friends, a meal, waking up in the morning. They can be important or special events, or just more run-of-the-mill moments. But whatever they are, when you can tackle them without smoking it will build up your confidence. It will also prove to you that you can do these things not smoking, and actually enjoy them. This data point will strengthen your resolve not to smoke. So while you may feel you want to put off quitting until after these challenging moments, it can be a mistake to do so because they give the most important kind of practical experience.

But does this advice work for everyone? Maybe for some people it's better to find a time when their schedule is clear so that they can wait for some days, weeks, or even months to pass to allow their brains and bodies to adjust before they face something difficult. Maybe it's better to tackle something like a holiday, big celebration with friends, or an important work deadline once someone has gone through withdrawal and their subconscious has readjusted a bit?

There are arguments both ways on this, and what works for one person may not work for another. But sometimes it helps to take a step back and look at things from a new perspective.

What would you say is the best time to improve your life? Isn't it right now? Why would you want to put an improvement off? Let's go back to the example of a cancer diagnosis and your two options for dealing with it. Imagine you've already made the only reasonable decision, which is to have the operation. Wouldn't you want to have that operation as soon as possible? Would you want to put it off for a single day? Wouldn't you want to get that cancer out of you, to start the healing process, to get on with your improved quality of life as soon as possible? Imagine if you opted for the operation and the doctor said that the soonest they could fit you in was in two years, and in the meantime you'd have to muddle through with the aspirin. Would you be pleased? Or utterly disappointed? You'd experience a hardship that could be have been avoided—a substantially reduced quality of life for two years. All the while your cancer continues to grow, so when you are finally able to have the operation the recovery time is even longer.

The fact is that there is only one good time to quit any drug: right now. The physical side won't get easier; it will only get progressively worse as your brain becomes increasingly proficient at countering the stimulating effects of the nicotine. The subconscious side will also adapt progressively as each and every inhalation hammers home still further to your subconscious the lesson that nicotine relieves stress and makes you feel better. As for your conscious mind, are you not at your strongest, most determined to stop right here and now? What do you have to gain in putting off the day you quit?

If you have a situation that feels tough to get through without smoking coming up in the next day or two, you get to test your mettle when you are at your strongest. It will give you a huge boost in confidence. And what if there's no definitive smoking situation coming up over the next few months? That's good, too! You can quit now and have time to get over the withdrawal and get used to not smoking before you have to deal with any major challenges.

The fact is, when you have changed your perception of smoking and you quit, then you aren't going to smoke again and your life is going to improve. It doesn't make any difference if the holiday with all your family is tomorrow or next year, if your next party is tonight or in six months, if your next meal out is next week or next year. Smoking is all about relieving a withdrawal; it's about feeling unpleasant, then feeling OK again. That same basic dynamic applies every time you smoke.

The biggest issue when you are quitting is dealing with cravings. We've already covered cravings in detail. Remember that it's a five-stage process: thought, fantasizing, anticipation, subconscious decision-making, and the search for excuses. Most people deal with cravings by trying not to even think about smoking. This isn't a viable tactic because it is not possible to stop yourself from thinking about smoking, particularly for the first few days or weeks when you are experiencing withdrawal. Your subconscious interprets withdrawal as "I need a smoke." The best time to disrupt the craving process is directly after the thought stage and before it hits the fantasizing stage. When the thought of a cigarette or a vape or dip enters your mind, don't start fantasizing about how wonderful it would be—see the reality.

Sure, you don't feel 100 percent and a cigarette will make you feel better. But it won't make you feel 100 percent, because it will also increase your heart rate and make you feel heavy and tired and weak. And it's not going to make you feel any better than you will in a few days if you just stick with it. Think of the cancer, and the option to have the operation or the aspirin. Smoking after you've quit is the equivalent of having the operation, going home to recover, then suddenly rushing back to the hospital and demanding that they put the cancer back in you because you don't fancy going through the recovery period right now.

Remember that fantasizing is exactly that—it's a fantasy. Avoiding it is as simple as keeping your thoughts grounded in reality. Remember the concept of maintenance cigarettes as opposed to the really "enjoyable" ones? When you think about smoking, think of those times you could smoke as much as you wanted and sat there wondering why on earth you kept putting them in your mouth and lighting them. The ones you really didn't enjoy but that you had to smoke anyway. Think of the tightness in your lungs, the accelerated heart rate, the cost, and the effect on your health. This is the reality of smoking. Don't be your own personal advertiser for the tobacco industry. Imagine an ad showing a happy, laughing smoker; imagine how ridiculous it would be seem. Don't work that con job on yourself. Reality, not fantasy, is the order of the day. Remember, fantasizing comes first, and if there's no fantasizing there can be no anticipation, no subconscious decision-making, and no panicked search for excuses.

See the withdrawal for exactly what it is; the death throes of Nicotine

Inc. The withdrawal is just their legal wrangling, their threatening letters, their clever tricks designed to keep you paying them money so that
they can survive and continue to control your life. But the fact is that it is,
and always has been, your decision about whether you pay up and keep
Nicotine Inc. alive, or withhold your payments and watch it die, no matter what tricks it comes up with to try to make you part with your hard-
earned cash.

One of the big problems with quitting nicotine is that the gains are
huge, but gradual. You don't feel different from one minute to the next, so
if you are not looking out for the positive shifts it is possible to miss them
entirely. Don't miss these gains; look out for them and notice them. The
lack of that heavy, drained feeling you get when you smoke and the feeling of your metal resilience returning day by day. Never take it for
granted, because it is an amazing feeling.

This period is sometimes referred to by addicts as "the pink cloud"
and is almost seen as a kind of temporary false high when you quit. It is
not temporary, and it is not false. It is that wonderful feeling of your brain
chemistry coming back to where it ought to be without outside interference, of your fitness returning. It can feel temporary—not because it
doesn't last, but because it very quickly becomes the norm and you can
quickly cease to appreciate it. More importantly, you can forget the degree to which smoking stole it from you. Remember that perfect house
you own that Nicotine Inc. repossessed? When you go back to living there
full time you can quickly take it for granted; the constant cleaning, re-
decorating, and general upkeep can be a bind. You can end up thinking
back fondly on those days when you had the option of getting away for a
bit, when you could pay a bit of money to Nicotine Inc. and they would let
you go somewhere nice and comfortable. You used to enjoy having that
chance to escape from the daily grind.

Wait, what?!

Can you see how false and nonsensical this sort of thinking is? And this is another point to bear in mind: after a short space of time your brain chemistry will get back to normal. The withdrawal will go. But if you smoke after you've gone through withdrawal, you won't even have the dubious pleasure of relieving the withdrawal. The nicotine will make you feel uptight, anxious, and out of sorts. It's a very similar feeling to having had too much caffeine. It isn't pleasant. The only reason people believe they enjoy smoking when they return to it after a week or so is because it ends the misery of the craving. But in purely physical terms it actually makes things worse. That first dose will never do what you think it will do anyway, and as soon as you've taken it your brain will start to recalibrate to counter the effects of the nicotine. When it starts to wear off you will suffer the same withdrawal that kept you imprisoned all those years. It's not a feeling your subconscious mind will ever forget; it will interpret that feeling as "I want a cigarette." You'll get no benefit whatsoever from that cigarette, but it will put you right back to square one in terms of quitting. It's like sitting in your house, thinking back fondly on those days when Nicotine Inc. used to give you a break from the daily grind . . . by allowing you to be exactly where you are now!

We've talked previously in this book about how there is no such thing as an addictive personality, only people whose coping mechanism is to consume something to change how they feel, and people who use other, more effective methods to deal with stress. You are about to quit something that will have become your main coping mechanism, be that smoking, vaping, or dipping. So you need to decide now what your next coping mechanism is going to be. If you want to live your best life, you need to leave the Alice in Wonderland way of coping—eating and drinking everything you come across in the hopes that it will solve your problems—and adopt healthier and more productive tools. The options are almost endless, but what you really need to ask yourself is "What do I enjoy?" or, more accurately for most people the question is, "What did I enjoy before I became obsessed with nicotine?"

Thinking about this can be a revelation. A lot of people, when they think back to before they started smoking, realize that they actually enjoyed sports. They don't enjoy it now, of course, because the elevated heart rate of a smoker makes exercise difficult and even deeply unpleasant. It can be quite a shock to realize how much your lifestyle has changed due to smoking. Exercise can be a great coping mechanism: it causes your brain to release endorphins (which makes you feel good); it helps you lose fat and gain muscle; and, perhaps most important of all, raises your natural resilience and confidence still further.

Remember how physical sickness and weakness make you want to hide away? And how health and strength make you want to get out there and seize the day? The healthier and stronger you are, the better you feel. Exercise may feel totally alien to you at the moment; you may look at people who run and go to the gym as absolute freaks, but that's only because you are heavy with nicotine. When you quit, the nicotine will soon wear off. Your heart rate will start to drop, your fitness will slowly return. At some point you may find that sitting around all day isn't actually that pleasant, that in fact you want to get out and take a walk. You may only exercise for a few minutes before you've had enough. But you may also find that you actually enjoy it, and that you feel better afterward, better than you have in a long time.

The next day, or a day or two later, you may get the urge again to just move your body out in the world. If you do it, and keep doing it, you'll find that over time your stamina will improve as your muscles adapt and strengthen. In time you'll be able to walk a bit farther, a bit faster. Walking isn't the only exercise, of course—you can run, swim, hit the gym, cycle, or play a team sport, so find what works for you. People who are healthy have a desire to exercise. Humans did not evolve to be sedentary, they evolved to *move*! This is an innate desire in us. It's only the drugs we take that rob us of that desire.

Some people are concerned that they will become addicted to exercise. One of our problems is that we tend to use the word "addiction" too widely. Addiction isn't about doing something repeatedly because it is both pleasurable and beneficial. Addiction is about being compelled to do something damaging, which is very different from doing something that is genuinely enjoyable and healthy and makes us feel good.

So exercise is a great coping mechanism and one that you shouldn't discount based on how you feel now (if you are still smoking). But there are lots of other ways to cope when you face challenges in life: a favorite show on TV, a night out with friends, playing a musical instrument, cooking, or another hobby or pastime that you used to enjoy. Some people find meditation helpful, which is essentially emptying your mind of everything and just enjoying a few minutes of peace and tranquility (which can be similar to what people do when they smoke a cigarette). But you can get a similar effect by losing yourself in a good book or film, or while listening to music, or getting absorbed in a hobby. All of these activities offer relief from the stresses and strains of life. Decide now what new coping mechanisms you will use when you have a bad day so that you have them in mind and easily accessible to you.

In chapter 21, we talked about the smokescreen or warped perception we've created to sugar-coat the image we have of ourselves as a smoker or vaper. We see ourselves as cool, rebellious, independent, instead of as a scared little child clinging to a security blanket, and poisoning ourselves in the process. But non-smokers do not see us as we see ourselves. They see smokers and vapers desperately gulping down lungfuls of a cancerous poison in a desperate attempt to alleviate their fear and becoming increasingly weak and exhausted in the process as well as paying ridiculous amounts of money for the privilege. They find the idea of spending hundreds of dollars on a vape or cigarettes laughable and pathetic. To them it's not cool and maverick, it's just a disgusting little comfort blanket.

Changing your self-image means not only changing how you see yourself, but also how you see other smokers and vapers. You are no longer going to be a nicotine addict. You don't need to start warping your perception, you just need to make an objective assessment. See it for what it is without all the hype and nonsense. Keep the actual facts in the forefront of your mind.

What we are talking about here is a drug. It's a drug that you happen to inhale as opposed to snorting or injecting or swallowing. It's a drug that makes you feel uptight and agitated before wearing off and leaving a corresponding feeling of being unfocused and out of sorts. Another dose of this drug will then relieve the out-of-sorts feeling, and herein lies the illusion of pleasure. Nicotine increases your heart rate, which makes physical activity increasingly difficult, and it upsets your appetite, making you far more likely to develop bad eating habits.

These are the simple chemical and physiological facts and deal only with the here and now, not to mention the other health risks that you can expect to cripple and then kill you farther down the line. This is what your smoking, vaping, or dipping boils down to with all the hype and nonsense stripped away.

This is the distilled essence of smoking, vaping, and dipping that needs to form the basis of your self-image. You are no longer someone who is being conned into paying large sums of money for a pathetic product that is destroying your health.

This chapter has covered seven essential principles. To review:

1. Mindset is important—Keep positive, but if you find yourself wavering or momentarily panicking, don't let it derail you. Just keep putting one foot in front of the other and keep making progress.

2. When should you quit?—Now!

3. You can deal with cravings—Every time the thought of a smoke, vape, or dip enters your mind, quash it immediately with the thought "I am

so lucky to be free of that horror." Don't dwell on it, don't reassess your decision to stop (that decision has been made and is irreversible). Try to think of a part of smoking or vaping that you particularly hated and whenever the thought enters your head, drag that image to the forefront and feel good that no matter what else is going on in your life right now, you have one massive gain to cheer you up: you never need to go through that again!

4. Don't miss the gains—Every day you will be improving, both physically and mentally. But remember, it isn't a straight path up; the path undulates. You may have good days and bad, and some days will be worse than the day before for various reasons. But overall there will be a steady improvement.

5. Coping mechanisms are key—Get your new, healthy coping strategies in place now so they are ready when you need them. Maybe it's getting out for a walk, listening to music, or calling a good friend to shift your mind when you feel a craving or are having a difficult day. Whatever works for you.

6. Change your self-image—See smoking and vaping as it really is, and see smokers and vapers as they really are. Redefine your self-image in light of this.

7. Physical withdrawal is part of the process—The second you put out your last cigarette, or exhale your last lungful of vape, you've done all you need to do physically to quit. But the withdrawal will now kick in. Whether you think of this withdrawal as your body and brain healing, or as you withholding payment from Nicotine Inc. until the organization dies from starvation of funds, or even that you've had an operation to remove a vile little tumor from your brain and you now

need some recovery time, you need to be aware that the withdrawal is going to kick in and your brain will interpret that feeling of the withdrawal as "I want a dose of nicotine." Think of it as though these thoughts are threatening letters from Nicotine Inc. to try to keep you in its clutches, or as signs your body and brain are healing from years of damage. You may feel out of sorts, disoriented, lethargic, restless, and dazed. It's not really any worse than having a touch of the flu for a few days, but you do need to know it's coming. And when it comes your brain will automatically trigger the thought: "Have a cigarette." This can be disconcerting when you are fired up and determined to stop. But the key is to expect this and to not let it derail you.

When you have these seven concepts in place, you are ready to quit. The next step is a simple enough thing, it's a thing you've done countless times before, usually without even thinking about it: light a cigarette, or inhale from your vape, or pack a lipful of dip. But this is going to be the most significant dose of nicotine you have taken since that first experimental dose, which had such massive, unintended consequences. This is going to be your last ever dose of nicotine.

When you take it, have it alone and somewhere quiet. Really concentrate on the whole experience. Think about how any minor pleasure is not a genuine gain, but something that has first been stolen from you, then partly returned. Feel how your heart rate accelerates and how this makes you feel heavy and weak. Imagine how it felt as a child to just run and run for the pure pleasure of it, about how nicotine has stolen this feeling from you without your even knowing it. Make a rough estimate of how much you've spent on your addiction over your lifetime. Think of what damage it's done to you already, physically and mentally. Think of those executives who head up those huge companies that your money has gone to and their seven- and eight-figure salaries. They reap the financial rewards while 480,000 Americans die every year and thirty times that number live with a serious smoking-related illness.

When you finish that final smoke, promise yourself that you will never, ever take another dose again. This time the decision is final and total. You may have made a similar promise several times in the past and broken it, but this time is different. Then, you didn't have the knowledge and understanding you need to succeed. Now you do. You will have good times and bad times ahead. It may be hard or it may be easy. But no one can force you to smoke, that is up to you and you alone, and since you know you are never going to smoke again you've already succeeded, you've already quit.

When that vow is made, know that it is irreversible, and it is set in stone. Never ever question it or doubt it. Questioning it can lead to craving, which, while not necessarily a sign you will fail to quit, will make life more difficult for you because you'll agonize over your decision and will be in that unpleasant mental spiral.

If you've already quit smoking, then needless to say, do not take more nicotine in order to go through this process, but you do still need to make a promise to never smoke again and to know that this is irreversible. You need to solidify in your mind that the decision has been made and can never be questioned or reversed.

Whenever the thought of smoking or vaping or dipping enters your mind from this point on, remember this moment. Remember that this was the time in your life that you analyzed nicotine, that you examined every single aspect of it individually and in immense detail. You reviewed the entire thing and decided you were done with it, once and for all. That decision is now done, made, and in the past, never to be questioned.

Mark this decision by taking your last dose of nicotine and making your vow. All you need to do then is to go on with your life and start to accrue, day by day, those massive life-changing benefits.

25.

The Path to Freedom

At this stage you should be both committed and prepared to quit, and it may be tempting to throw this book to one side and get out there and start enjoying your fabulous new life. But it's worth taking some time at this stage to look at how change works, particularly how we change our behavior.

There are four stages in the process of changing a negative behavior that we think we enjoy:

Asleep Stage

This is when we are unaware that we even have a problem. Think back to when you first started smoking or vaping. You were younger than you are now, fitter than you are now, you could probably take it or leave it for a bit. Maybe you only smoked occasionally, when you went out on the weekend, or on certain occasions. As we've covered, this stage never lasts forever, but while you're in it you don't even think of your nicotine consumption as a problem. You think you're not like all those other idiots who have to smoke all day, every day—you're the one person who managed to buck the trend!

This stage is also known as "unconscious incapable," because you are not conscious of the problem and are therefore incapable of rectifying it. In your conscious mind your smoking or vaping simply isn't a problem, and because it isn't a problem you can't do anything about it. After all, how can you go about fixing a problem you aren't even aware of?

Aware Stage

This is when you start to realize that you have a problem. Just as time passing seems to kind of happen while we're busy living our lives, so too addiction slowly takes hold. One moment we are sampling that first, experimental cigarette, and because we have no concept or experience of addiction, we simply cannot imagine how it could be possible that we could need this thing all day, every day. It's such an alien idea to us that we have no fear of the substance. We're incapable of treating it with the fear it deserves because fear requires knowledge; we need to truly understand the horrors that await us. It's like the false courage of ignorance compared to the true courage of experience as described by Cyril McNeile, the World War I veteran and author. The courage displayed by the soldiers who had experienced the horrors and indiscriminate death of the front and still returned to fight was a very different form of courage to those soldiers who were going out to fight for the first time with visions of glory and excitement. If you have never experienced something, you are incapable of allotting to it the respect it deserves. It is not a failing, it is just the reality of life as a human being. For this reason, no matter how many times we're warned of the dangers of smoking, many of us still sample that first, experimental dose of nicotine.

For a short period, of course, everything is fine. We don't need to smoke all the time, in fact, we can pretty much take it or leave it. For many, whatever fear of smoking we did harbor actually dissipates when we try our first cigarette. We've been told it's addictive, but initially that's not our experience. We believe that we're the one person who has managed to stay in control.

The problem is that as time passes we do get hooked. We start to enjoy it more and more as the physical side kicks in, and our desire for it increases until we simply can't do without it. In the same way that we can become aware of the years passing, perhaps on a certain birthday, or on the New Year, or realizing that it's been many years since an event that is fresh in our mind actually occurred, so we suddenly realize that we're hooked. What was once something we could take or leave is suddenly a necessity.

When I was young, I used to smoke only when I was out with friends. It felt nice and simple, and I felt so clever because I'd played the house and won! I'd put away any cigarettes I had left over until the following week. But then there would be a day when my parents were both out, I'd be at home alone while those cigarettes just sat there, singing their siren song, so I'd have one. Soon I started looking forward to them going out so that I could have that smoke, and if their plans changed and they stayed home, I felt robbed! I'd go out for a walk so I could have that smoke. After all, I felt as though it was due to me anyway. Pretty soon, I was going out for walks every day, and I remember being infuriated if my parents decided they'd join me for my evening stroll.

Everyone's experience is different in some ways, and yet the same in others. The exact way the trap closes will be different for each person, but for every person the trap does close, eventually. It's like the children's game of tag called Mr. Wolf. When you start the game the "wolf" is so far away from you can't even imagine how he or she could close the gap. But eventually, you turn around and the wolf has caught up to you. From afar, addiction is no more than a vague concept, an ill-defined idea. But all too soon you are in its grasp.

This is the second stage, which is marked by being "conscious incapable." That is, we are conscious of the problem, but we are incapable of doing anything about it. We're hooked, we're stuck, but we can't imagine changing. Every time we try to quit we are miserable, more miserable then when we're smoking, so we make the seemingly logical choice and keep going back to it.

Awake Stage

In the awake stage, we possess the desire to change, and we've also acquired the knowledge to actually put this shift into place. The goal of this book is to take you to the awake stage by giving you the knowledge and tools to make the change that you want to make. You know there is a problem, but now you possess the ability to actually do something about it. You are "conscious capable" because you are not only aware of the problem, but you are capable of rectifying it.

This is where most programs stop. After all, this is the stage when you quit, which is what you're after, right? You're conscious of the problem and you're able to do something about it. Job done, right? Well, not necessarily, because there is another stage:

Alive Stage

In this stage, we are "unconscious capable." We are unconscious of the problem because the problem is solved, it's done with, and we're now getting on with the rest of our lives. The main differentiating factor between the awake and alive stages is that during "awake" we are consciously doing something about the problem. When we are in the "alive" stage of smoking we are consciously ensuring that the thought of smoking doesn't become a craving, we are reminding ourselves how the whole thing was an elaborate con, and how happy we are to be free. But at some point we move from "awake," where we consciously stop smoking, to "alive," where we no longer need to consciously stop. It happens automatically. Our subconscious does that for us. So "awake" is when the subconscious is triggering us to smoke and we are jumping in with our conscious mind to stop that happening, while "alive" is when our conscious mind catches up and starts seeing the reality of smoking. It is here that our mind becomes one. Both our conscious and subconscious are on the same page, telling us:

DON'T SMOKE!

Most people will pick this book up while they are in stage two: aware. They know they have a problem but they don't know what to do about it, so they hope this book will be the silver bullet they've been looking for. In fact, these stages don't really have any clear delineation; there is a lot a gray between each stage. Some people may be vaping away, fairly happy with it, but just starting to feel in the back of their minds that it's creeping into their lives a bit too much. Others may be fairly content with their smoking or vaping and want to read this mostly out of curiosity. These two examples are in the gray area between stage one to stage two. Still others may be between stages two and three; they may already be wrestling with some of the ideas we've provided in this book and already on the journey of acquiring the knowledge required to do something about their smoking.

The purpose of this book is to take you from wherever you are to stage four, not just stage three. The information we have provided so far has given you the knowledge to move from stage two to stage three, in other words it has given you the knowledge to eradicate your nicotine addiction. This is a good result, right? But hang on, do we want good, or do we want excellent? How do we get from awake to alive, how do we get from good to excellent?

The most obvious answer is time. The more you do something, the more proficient you get, and, as we've covered in this book, the more you do the same thing over and over again, the quicker your subconscious will automate the processes involved. So everyone who's in stage three will eventually move to stage four. But is there a way we can hurry the process along a bit?

In fact, there is. There have been studies that show that while repetition is the key to creating new habits, we can create new habits more quickly if we feel positive emotions when we are performing them. This isn't exactly rocket science, it's as simple as this: if you're enjoying doing something, it becomes easier and easier to do it regularly.

How do you think it was so easy (in fact almost impossible to avoid) to start smoking so much in the first place? It is because nicotine addiction fools us into thinking that each smoke is enjoyable. It really is that simple. So to master quitting smoking, you need to try to enjoy not smoking. So how do you do this?

As we've discussed, one important piece is to start seeing smoking and vaping and dipping as exactly what they are: things that give nothing (other than to partially restore what they have already taken) and take so much. When we see this completely and thoroughly, giving up the behavior becomes an absolute pleasure. This is all about mindset.

It's useful at this point to differentiate between "mindset" and "positive thinking." Positive thinking conjures images of people telling themselves something over and over again in the hopes that they will eventually believe it. This may work for some, but it never worked for me. If someone tells me something I don't believe, I don't believe it. I don't believe it whether they say it to me once or a thousand times, and it makes no difference if it's me telling myself the lie or if it's someone else telling me.

Mindset, however, is what you genuinely believe about something. Remember in chapter 1, we talked about how our beliefs aren't necessarily reality, and (hard as it can sometimes seem) we can change our beliefs? Changing our beliefs requires analysis, understanding, and clarity. This is what it means to change our mindset. Telling yourself over and over that you don't want to smoke doesn't do you any good at all if you *do* want to smoke, in the same way that telling yourself that you are a billionaire when you're stone-cold broke won't alter your bank balance. But actually changing your mindset, changing your core beliefs about smoking and vaping, that really does make a difference, because then you genuinely don't want to smoke. And when you get to that stage, stopping becomes enjoyable and you minimize the transition period between "awake" and "alive."

Remember that mindset is not a constant. One day you may be over the moon, happy to have stopped and wondering why it took you so long, and the next you may find yourself suddenly miserable and unhappy. The key is to stick with it, keep in mind all that we've covered in this book, keep on keeping on whether it's easy or hard, because it will get progressively easier as time goes by. And if you can enjoy the process while you're doing it, see all the positives, then you make the process quicker and easier. Concentrate on the return of your mental resilience, your joy and happiness, your fitness levels, your energy, and your freedom. If you focus on the positives and really enjoy quitting as much as you can, it will get that much easier that much quicker.

26.

Pay It Forward

One of the main issues with quitting nicotine is that it's gradual and negative, and by negative I mean the benefit comes not from doing, but from not doing something. Over the next few days, weeks, and months you will start to feel better and better; better than you ever did when you were smoking, better even than you felt smoking that first cigarette of the day. You will feel lighter, stronger, calmer, more competent, and able to deal with life on its own terms. You probably won't feel much different from one moment to the next, but those improvements are happening to you, indeed they are starting right now as the nicotine begins to leave your system, never to be replaced.

This can feel strange in a way; often when we work toward something amazing we have something tangible to show for it, a new gadget, a new item, a certificate of achievement. With quitting drugs, it's the absence of a thing that is the achievement that is to be celebrated. It can hit you at odd times: no longer will you be leaving home thinking, "Keys, wallet (or purse), phone, cigarettes, and lighter (or vape)." Now it's just "Keys, wallet (or purse), and phone." See this for what it is, not a pleasure that is missing, but a weight that has been hanging around your neck for however many years you've been smoking. A weight that's been dragging you down and ruining your life. It wasn't something you ever chose. All you did was what untold millions who have gone before you have done: you were curious and so took that first experimental puff. That was the only thing you chose, the rest was forced upon you. Now you have made a conscious decision—to quit once and for all. You've stopped drifting and you've taken back control.

As you slowly heal, as your body and brain recover, as your physical strength and fitness levels return, you can get on with your life and enjoy it as much as you can. You'll have good days and bad days, but the bad days will be less likely to totally derail you, and the good days will be even better.

Take your time; adjust to your new life. Enjoy breaking all of the associations. It was a game for me, doing something I couldn't have imagined without a smoke and enjoying it more than before. It reinforces my resolve and fills me with gratitude.

You may have doubts, lingering cravings, or times of disbelief. That's all OK; don't worry. Worrying about it will just make it worse. Just accept it. You are the only one who can make yourself smoke and you aren't going to do that, so whatever comes along is irrelevant. Just observe it, pretend you're a scientist watching something happening from the outside, watching with academic interest but no emotional involvement.

Take care of yourself; you deserve it. One day in the very near future, when you feel at peace and whole, perhaps your gratitude will overflow. There is incredible power in giving to someone else the gift you have been given, in helping someone else become free. It is an amazing and life-affirming thing to help another person. Either individually or by joining me in this movement, let's ensure that we and our children understand the true nature of nicotine. There is so much to be done, from simply helping one person to getting in touch and spreading the word.

Helping other people is one of life's great secrets to happiness. Compassion is actually quite selfish. The Dalai Lama said in a TV interview on ABC News, "The practice of compassion is ultimately to benefit you. So I usually say: We are selfish, but be wise selfish (helping others) rather than foolish selfish (only helping yourself)."

Exercising compassion and helping other people is incredibly satisfying. Brain scans show that acts of kindness register in our brain's pleasure centers much like eating chocolate does. The same pleasure centers in the brain light up when we get a gift as when we donate to charity. Helping others ultimately helps you. It is an amazing and completely natural high. Over and over it has been shown that service to others is a vital part of our happiness as humans.

Do it. Pay it forward. Go gently and remember never to judge. Change starts here, change starts now, and you are the most important part of this change. The world needs you to be your best. The world needs you to help save it, one person at a time. At the end of the day, *This Naked Mind* is about a mind that comes to care for and respect itself, just as it is, just as it came into this world—simply naked. Remove the pollutants you struggle with. When we do that, we save ourselves and prepare this amazing planet and all its incredible inhabitants for the next generation, for our children.

Pay it forward; it's your turn.

P.S. We hope you enjoyed this book. To explore other habits and addictions, visit: AlcoholExplained.com or ThisNakedMind.com.

Acknowledgments

Thank you:

Allen Carr—who paved the way for us, as he did for many others.

Thad A. Polk, PhD—whose neurological insight into the cycle of addiction allows us to better understand the cycles of craving and reward.

Dave Gray, the author of *Liminal Thinking*—whose unique and methodical approach to changing beliefs informed this work.

Dr. BJ Fogg—who confirmed what we already knew: lasting change stems from emotion.

Dr. Caroline Leaf—whose dedication to research allows us to understand our brains better.

From William:

Eddie and Elvis. Eddie, for the games of football and the conversations about food. Elvis, for the walks in Gunnersbury Park and the conversations about Judge Dredd.

Stacy. My left-hand man.

El; for everything, the constant organization and effort to keep a house in order and a family happy, which is always taken for granted.

From Annie:

Kiddos & husband; you are the best, always.

And to my ladies who keep me grounded, well dressed, and constantly laughing.

Also by the Authors